A Hundred
Autumn Leaves

A Hundred Autumn Leaves

The *Ogura Hyakunin Isshu*:
Translated and Annotated

Sagnik Bhattacharya

PARTRIDGE
A Penguin Random House Company

To order additional copies of this book, contact
Partridge India
000 800 10062 62
orders.india@partridgepublishing.com

www.partridgepublishing.com/india

Dedicated to
All my teachers and my parents,
Susmita and Tonmoy
Bhattacharya.

Acknowledgment

In this attempt to present the Ogura Hyakunin Isshu to the ordinary and lay English readers, I have been amply helped by a large number of people and not acknowledging their contributions would be a sin on my part which I do not wish to commit.

I am grateful to Professor Joshua Scott Mostow, Associate Head of the Department of Asian Studies, University of British Columbia, Canada who has provided me the permission for using his extraordinary book *"Pictures of the Heart: The Hyakunin Isshu in Word and Image"* as a source of information wherever required in the course of interpreting the poems.

I would also like the thank the University of Virginia Library for granting me the permission to print the original Japanese poems of the Hyakunin Isshu as well as to use Clay McCauley's translation of the hundred poems for comparison.

I am also thankful to Ms. Samprikta Pal, Assistant professor of English, Government General Degree College, Singur, University of Burdwan, for editing this book and rendering support and encouragement throughout the course of its development.

Finally, I would like to acknowledge the the support from my parents and especially the help from my mother Susmita Bhattacharya who has undertaken the task of illustrating some of the poems of this book and my father Tonmoy Bhattacharya, who has made the book possible.

Introduction

"The Hundred Poets, One Poem Each" of Ogura mountain is perhaps the most famous of all the poetic anthologies of medieval Japan. Yet, such is the irony that it was never meant to be used in the way it is, in the recent years. Each and every educated man is Japan is familiar with at least a few of the poems included here, and however humble it be, every house possesses a copy of the text. But it is particularly known for the card game called *Karuta or Ota-garuta (Karuta* comes from the Portuguese word for card *Carta.)* among the Japanese populace of today, instead of as an anthology compiled for a very specific purpose which we shall come to discuss in a short while.

In those days, Japan's aristocratic class was perhaps the most sophisticated when compared to the same around the world. Composing poems was not a leisurely activity and more that a favorite pass-time for the nobility. It was specifically a court activity, especially in the Heian period. During this Heian period, beginning from 794 CE, Japan entered into a period of prolonged peace and unprecedented stability--both political as well as economic. Thus, literary arts, cultural etiquette, and leisurely activities such as poetry writing got a huge impetus that somewhat lacked in the Nara and Yamato periods. The capital was shifted to Heian-kyo (*Abode of Peace*, present Kyoto), and this became the centre of all literary activities, and we shall find, that all the hundred poets of this anthology have some relation to this imperial city. And now, when poetry, especially court-poetry received the royal patronage and support, composing *waka,* or Japanese poems became almost an epidemic affecting the nobility all across the capital. It was during this time that compiling poems into anthologies was also felt to be important, and even this received the royal sanction. The *Manyoshu* compiled in 759 CE is the largest and the oldest of all Japanese anthologies. Other anthologies include the *Kokin Wakashu,* the *Gosenshu* and of course the *Hyakunin Isshu.* However, it will be wrong to say that there is merely one 'Hyakunin Isshu.' It was a sort of a trend for the aristocrats of that time to compile their own 'Hundred poems by hundred people' and all of them were named "Hyakunin Isshu." But the *Ogura* Hyakunin Isshu is by far the most famous of all them all because of the vast period of history that it captures through its poems as well as because of its current popularity.

Mount Ogura

Mount Ogura, now called Arashiyama is a mountain of about 2,000 meter height located between Kitaaki and Minamiaki villages in the Nagano Prefecture of Japan to the northern side of the Hozu river-gorge and to the western side of Kyoto.

This mountain, has for a long period of time, been associated with the literary world of medieval as well as later Japanese literature. In the Heian period it won the epithet "Poet's Mount." Heian court-poets sang to its beauty and it was almost immortalized due to this particular text, the Ogura Hyakunin Isshu. The later literary genius Matsuo Basho wrote the "Saga Diary" on the foothills of this mountain. It is also associated with the famous "poetry immortal" Saigyo who built his first hermitage there.

Now, if we come to discuss the purpose of the composition, it is necessary to clarify, that it was not created by royal order or sanction. It was compiled when a nobleman, Fujiwara no Tame'ie, asked his poet father, to arrange for a hundred poems to decorate the screens of the palace near Ogura mountain that he was furnishing for his father-in-law. His father, a poet and a poetry-expert, Fujiwara no Teika, thus produced the *Ogura Hyakunin Isshu*. This information is found from Teika's own diaries the *Meigetsuki*. During this time, writing and maintaining personal diaries became a fashion among the literate population. Mount Ogura, it seems has long been the inspiration for poets and occupied an important position in the lives of many a poet. The following is one of the many poems referring to Mount Ogura. A poem by Yoshihiro Tsuchida reads:

> To Ogura I have come,
> And at the hill I have gazed.
> Every dawn and dusk.
>
> Reliving those mountain paths
> I once walked as a child.

Fujiwara no Teika

Perhaps his fate was his fortunate birth into the illustrious Fujiwara clan, a family of renowned poets of great fame, that made a poet out of him. Whatever it be, being born as a Fujiwara had its benefits, especially at a time when that clan had practically monopolized the entire bureaucracy at the Imperial court. His grandfather was Fujiwara no Toshitada and his father was Shunzei (of poem 83). As a youth, Teika was a sickly boy but as the eldest son, he was obligated to carry on the family legacy. Unfortunately due to complex court politics, Teika was overlook for much of his early life. However after a fortunate turn of events, he was noticed by Emperor Go-Toba (poem 99) who eventually commissioned him to compile two new anthologies including the *Shin Kokin Waka-shu*.

Over time though, Teika and Emperor Gotoba came to disagree over poetry and the anthology, leading to an increasingly distant and cold relationship. Teika found Gotoba dictatorial, while Gotoba didn't care for Teika's free writing style. At times, Teika and Gotoba openly criticized one another in their poems, or in their diaries, and eventually Gotoba banished Teika for a year. Teika however, became closer to Gotoba's son who later became Emperor Juntoku (poem 100). Although Gotoba became increasingly occupied with the martial arts, and with wresting power back from the samurai rulers in Kamakura, Teika enjoyed juntoku's generous patronage.

Unfortunately for Emperor Gotoba, his imperial forces were completely destroyed by the Kamakura army, and Gotoba was sent into exile (since it was not permissible to kill the Emperor) along with his immediate family. Teika was not involved in the war, so he remained in Kyoto, and even reached the Imperial post of Middle Counselor. During this time, he also completed another Imperial anthology, the Shin Chokusen Wakashū, which shows more of his later down-to-earth style.

Finally though, his health declined from old age and from the famine at the time, he retired and took Buddhist tonsure. It was during his final years in a Buddhist monastery that he was invited by his son's father-in-law,

Lord Utsunomiya no Yoritsuna, to his villa in Mount Ogura near Kyoto.

According to an alternative source, Lord Utsunomiya asked Teika to compile 100 poems in his own hand, so that they could be adorned on the silk screens of his villa, and these 100 eventually became the collection that we know today.

Fujiwara's style of poetry was very allusive and readers often miss the subtle references that are relevant as well as important in understanding the "'true" meaning of the poem as meant by Teika himself.

Major Themes

Major themes of the hundred poems of the anthology are, nature, separation and longing, beauty, and of course the most popular theme--seasons. These themes appear frequently, but cannot be said to be repetitive. And it must also not be assumed that other themes do not appear in the text. The first two poems, are about the nature of rule of emperors and empresses, the seventh poem is about home-sickness, the eleventh laments the poets banishment. There are a certain major or rather somewhat characteristic themes in the this anthology which are also the characteristic themes for poetry in Heian Japan. We shall discuss a few in details and leave the rest for the contemplation of the reader.

When we speak of Love as a frequent theme in the Hyakunin Isshu, we need to understand an important aspect of Japanese thought. This is the concept of *"mono no aware"* or the "pathos for things" that is, the pity for the transient nature of life and all things around us. It is sometimes also equated with the European concept of *"memento mori"* or Reminder of Death, but there is still no exact interpretation of this word in English. Even after severe debate, scholars have failed to ascertain whether this concept came to Japan with the arrival and thriving of Buddhism or was it an idea indigenous to Japanese thought; anyhow, this thought, and particularly this phrase is very common in Japanese literature and is most prominently found in the "Tale of Genji", a novel by Murasaki Shikibu, who is also the poet of the 57th poem. This very phrase is found no less that a thousand and eight times in the entire original work. Thus scholars believe the whole idea, or the whole view conveyed through the "Tale of Genji" is all about the impermanence of life. So, when we speak of love, longing, separation and reunion in the case of Japanese poetry, they all portray a sort of happiness as well as sorrow. When it, is love or reunion, the poet fears that it will soon pass away and be, but a distant memory. When it is separation or longing, he does not complain or curse his fate; he merely enjoys the moments that he spends waiting and shedding tears for he knows that the time will come when reunion will take place and this sorrow will give way to a far greater joy but then he will again be counting his days in fear of separation again. So, the underlying tone of almost the entire text is that of melancholy and sorrow yet there is a wish to find an end to this sorrow and an equally strong one to enjoy this pain.

This feeling finds prominent place in the Love poems of the Ogura Hyakunin Isshu which comprise a major section of the anthology. Among the various types of love poems, a common essence in it, is the cruelty of a lover like Poem number 82:

Though in deep distress
Through your cruel blow, my life
Still is left to me.

But I cannot keep my tears;
They break forth from my grief.

Courtesy: Clay McCauley

The poets of Heian Japan used another beautiful technique in their love poems particularly. They blended seasonal warmth and coldness with feelings of love; they used seasons in a reference for comparison.

In the mountain village,
it is in winter that my loneliness
increases most,
when I think how both have dried up,
the grasses and people's visits.

Courtesy: Clay McCauley

Even in the seventeenth poem, the metaphor of the flowing of the river dyed in red refers to the imparting of the feeling of love unto his lover by him or perhaps vice-versa, and then he uses another rhetorical device of ancient poetry, a divine or rather metaphysical comparison. He says, "even when the gods held sway in ancient lands" he wants to immortalize his love and claim it as uncomaparable in all history and even in the divine world.

In case of love poems, we might consider the following reasons for their abundance in, not only the Ogura

Hyakunin Isshu, but in general all Japanese poetry. Courtship in Nara and Heian Japan was very popular and it was almost considered an etiquette do it in the proper and most dignified way. This demanded poetry. In Japanese society of that time, it was customary for men to spend the night with a lover and after leaving her chamber, send a note proclaiming his love to her, typically written on a paper fan. When sending it with the help of a servant, it is obvious that the requirement to conceal the message in metaphors was greatly felt by these men. After receiving the note, the lady, was expected to write a reply exactly in the meter of the former poem and send it back to the man. This way poetry actually grew out to become one of the favourite pass-times, a socio-cultural etiquette of the upper as well as the middle class (not largely for the Peasants though). This custom also somewhat contributed to the sheer number of *wakas* or Japanese poems dating back to the Heian and Nara periods as well as its development. Moreover, in the Nara and Heian periods, the militarization of the society had not begun yet, which dawned with the Kamakura period; and thus, expression of love through poetry, or rather the very art of composing poetry by the court nobles was not proscribed, instead, encouraged. The *Bushi-do* or the "Way of the Warrior", a code of conduct followed by the Samurai, looked down upon these arts and men indulging in them were said to "resemble a woman."

Next the most abundant theme is the 'Seasons.' The seasons mainly explored here are Autumn, Spring, Summer and Winter in order of frequency. Autumn is the most picturesque of all he seasons in Japanese poetry along with Spring. In both the cases of Autumn and Spring, we find a sense of melancholy and a feeling of being forsaken prevails in the tone of the poems. This may be well-justified in case of autumn, when we consider a country where the winters are severe and disrupt normal life. Autumn presents a season of retreating warmth. This is when the imaginative poet finds himself feeling forsaken and abandoned and thus craves for company, with this very tone, the poet says:

> In the mountain depths,
> Treading through the crimson leaves,
> The wandering stag calls.
>
> When I hear the lonely cry,
> Sad--how sad!--the autumn is.

Courtesy: Clay McCauley

It is also a season when the thoughts are said to be deserting the poet, because the period of winter will also bring a period of absolute dormancy, perhaps even dormancy of thoughts like in the following poem:

> As I view the moon,
> Many things come into my mind,
> And my thoughts are sad;
>
> Yet it's not for me alone,
> That the autumn time has come.

Courtesy: Clay McCauley

But, surely Spring should present itself with more jocund thoughts, being a season that heralds the warm summer, and a season of flowers and wellness. So is the case with some poems like the one from the *Kokin Wakashu* that says:

Naniwa-tsu ni,	In Naniwa's marsh,
Sakuya kono hana,	The Flowers blossom again,
Fuyu gomo ri,	Lying dormant through all winter.
Ima wu haru be to,	But now it is Spring,
Sakuya kono hana	And the flowers blossom again.

But Spring is also sometimes looked upon with a sense of melancholia that is not befitting its nature and grandeur. When we look at some poems from outside the Hyakunin Isshu, we find words like "haru wa kanashiki" or Sad Spring. This is again re-invoking the principle of *mono no aware*, here the poet does not honestly think that the Spring is "sad", like he did for autumn, instead here he actually laments the fact that the Spring will soon be over and from this fear lurking beneath his thoughts, he says that he pities the spring, because it is so transient.

However, I would like to take the liberty to explain another purpose of the poem just quoted from the Kokin Wakashu, that is, it is generally believed that this poem was written to celebrate the accession of the Emperor Nintoku to the imperial throne after an interregnum of three years. So, the coming of Spring signifies the return of the emperor, and the blossoming of cherry is the wish for a prosperous reign. By this example, the reader by now have an idea of the nature of the poems, that are included in this anthology.

They often have at least two, in some cases as many as three different meanings. So, this single poem of Naniwa Bay can be interpreted as a seasonal poem, a love poem or even a poem to celebrate the reign of the ruler.

On the other hand, Winter is associated with the feeling of being forsaken and left alone, the typical imagery for winter is haze, snow storm, frost, and the colour white.

> At the break of day,
> Just as though the morning moon
> Lightened the dim scene,
>
> Yoshino's village lay
> In a haze of falling snow.

Courtesy: Clay McCauley

(In this particular poem, the reference to the morning moon refers to the whiteness and loneliness of winter and this poem also stands as an example of feelings mixed with seasons.)

Whereas Autumn is red or rather orange with a slight tint of yellow and as John Keats described it: "A season of mellow fruitfulness" and of drying leaves. Spring, is red, and pink in color mixed with certain shades of green; typically the season of Flowers.

Altogether, there are 43 poems in the Hyakunin Isshu that cover the topics of Love and the Seasons.

Style and Tradition

The Ogura Hyakunin Isshu has a hundred poems written by a hundred poets. Most of whom are court nobles, emperors and empresses. However it will be wrong to assume that the names of others, that is commoners are not found here, but their number in relatively negligible. All of these hundred poems are called *"Tanka"*, that is a short poem composed in 31 syllables spread across five lines. The first three lines have 5 and 7 syllables alternately making up 17 syllables just as a Haiku would have had. Then, another two lines each of 7 syllables are added, making up a total of 31. This structure is very important when dealing with Japanese poetry or *"waka"* as they are called. When trying to understand, *tankas* we must first understand Waka, that is the general term used to mean poems written particularly in the Japanese language. Wakas began as early as in 750 AD with "short poems" called 'Tanka' and longer ones called 'Choka.' This is the nomenclature used in the Manyoshu(759 AD)--the oldest collection of Japanese poems. Among the five lines, the first three, which are the in the same scheme of composition as haiku, are called *kami-no-ku (upper phrase)* and the lower two of seven syllables each are called *shimo-no-ku (lower phrase)*. Tanka became so popular in Japan during the medieval years, that the term Tanka became equated with the general word *waka* itself.

In ancient times, it was a custom between two writers to exchange waka instead of letters in prose. In particular, it was common between lovers. Reflecting this custom, five of the twenty volumes of the Kokin Wakashū gathered waka for love. In the Heian period the lovers would exchange waka in the morning when lovers met at the woman's home. The exchanged waka were called *Kinuginu*, because it was thought the man wanted to stay with his lover and when the sun rose he had almost no time to put on his clothes on which he had lain instead of a mattress (it being the custom in those days). Works of this period, *The Pillow Book* and *The Tale of Genji* provide us with such examples in the life of aristocrats. Murasaki Shikibu uses 795 waka in her *The Tale of Genji* as waka that her characters made in the story. Some of these are her own, although most are taken from existing sources. Shortly, making and reciting waka became a part of aristocratic culture. They recited a part of appropriate waka freely to imply something on an occasion.

Much like the elaborate tea ceremony, there were a number of rituals and events surrounding the composition, presentation, and judgment of waka. There were two types of waka contests that produced occasional poetry: *Utakai* and *Utaawase*. Utakai was a party in which all participants wrote a waka and recited them. Utakai derived from Shikai, Kanshi party and was held in occasion of public gatherings like seasonal party for the New Year, celebrations for a newborn baby, a birthday, or a newly built house. *Utaawase* was a contest in two teams. Themes were determined, and a chosen poet from each team wrote a waka for a given theme. The judge appointed a winner for each theme and gave points to the winning team. The team which received the largest sum was the winner. The first recorded Utaawase was held in around 885 AD. At first, Utaawase was playful and mere entertainment, but as the poetic tradition deepened and grew, it turned into a serious aesthetic contest, with considerably more formality.

Female Poets in the Anthology

This poetry writing tradition is also found among the female poets of the Hyakunin Isshu, though 79 of the poems are written by men, there are 21 female poets in the found here as well. Most of these poets are found between poem numbers 55 to 65, but they are also scattered around casually in the chronological order. Many of these women represent the first female authors in world history including Lady Murasaki who wrote the Tales of Genji and her famous diary, and Sei Shonagon who authored the Pillow Book.

Poetry in the days of the ancient Heian Court was everywhere and women wrote poetry as much as men did if not more. Like men, they participated in Imperial contests as well and made a name for themselves. Not surprisingly, some of these have been preserved in the Hyakunin Isshu, just as they were in official Imperial anthologies, such as the Kokin Wakashū. However, one interesting custom to note is that the women poets never used their own name. Instead they often used sobriquets associated with where their family was affiliated with, or their position in the Court. Lady Izumi's father was governor of Izumi province for example.

Murasaki Shikibu is the most famous of all the poets included in the Hyakunin Isshu and the following poem numbered 57 was composed by her:

> I truly do not know, back then
> If He had crossed my path,
> For a gloomy cloud had hid the Moon
> And cast a shade upon the earth.

The headnote of this poem describes the experience of one night when Lady Murasaki had seen someone she had known long ago, but she only saw him or her in the passing as he or she raced by. But there are many interpretations as to who that person was. Many believe it was a fellow female acquaintance while others wonder if it was a male lover. Unfortunately we can't be sure.

Lady Murasaki, known as Murasaki Shikibu in Japanese, was a somewhat unusual figure in the 11th century Heian Court, both for her talents and her personality. Compared to other women of that era, like Lady Izumi (poem 56) who was very passionate, and Sei Shonagon (poem 62) who was very bold Lady Murasaki was more withdrawn and sullen and prone to be alone, or exchange letters with other women who shared her melancholy.

Lady Murasaki was among those rare women at the time who learned to read Classical Chinese, which normally was used by men of the Heian Court for official purposes, Buddhist literature, and of course Chinese-style poetry or *Kanshi* and literature. Women generally did not learn it, though the women listed above were exceptions. Indeed, Lady Murasaki's father, Fujiwara no Tametoki, was said to have lamented that Lady Murasaki was born a woman, because her talents for literature was outstanding. In any case, it was Lady Murasaki's talents that led her to being recruited as a lady-in-waiting to Empress Shoshi along with other dynamic women of her generation.

Unfortunately, we know very little about Lady Murasaki today, apart from her writings: the Tales of Genji, her poetry, and of course her diary which covers a year or two of her life while serving the powerful Fujiwara no Michinaga. I've explored her poetry in my annotation at length, so we need not cover it here. We don't even know her real name. The term murasaki (紫, meaning "purple") refers to one of her characters in the Tales of Genji, her most famous work of fiction.

The next most famous of all court poets of Heian Japan was Lady Izumi or Izumi Shikibu, a woman of caliber as great as Lady Murasaki. Izumi Shikibu was a mid Heian period Japanese poet. She is a member of the Thirty-six Medieval Poetry Immortals. She was the contemporary of Murasaki Shikibu, and Akazome Emon at the court of empress Joto Mon-In. Her life of love and passion earned her the nickname of The Floating Lady from Michinaga. Her poetry is characterized by passion and sentimental appeal. Her style was the direct opposite of that of Akazome Emon, even though both served in the same court and were close friends. At the court she also nursed a growing rivalry withMurasaki Shikibu, who had a similar poetic style, though this rivalry pales in comparison with Murasaki Shikibu's spirited competition with Sei Shōnagon. Izumi Shikibu's emotional poetry won her the praises at the court, people of great renown including Fujiwara no Kinto could not help but admire her poetry.

As a personal comment, it may be noticed that the female poets in the anthology, through are few in number, are much more profound in influence. That is, their style of poetry is much more affecting than that of the men. The female poets seem to involve the other partner in a sort of conversation through the poem, instead of adopting a more didactic or statementing attitude to express their love.

History, Society and Culture

The four islands to the extreme east of Asia, spreading from north to south in a concave manner hosted human settlement since about 200,000 BCE. The lush ecosystem of the islands actively supported human settlement that is definitely known to have existed since the last ice age. A paleolithic culture existed in Japan from about 32,000 BC. But the first proper historical period of Japan traced from pottery sources is the *Jomon* period that is the name given to the period from 14000 BCE till about 300 BCE. A fairly large number of hunting-gathering men populated these islands that were, still connected with the rest of Asia. Spreading over more that 10,000 years, the Jomon culture gradually made way for a newer form of society; brought about by a social revolution in and around 400 BCE. This new culture came to be called the *"Yayoi* Period" that lasted from 400 BCE to about 250 BCE. During this time, new technological inventions were brought about revolutionizing the sphere of agriculture as well as artistic productions. Shortly after this period, in the first century AD, Japan is for mentioned as a kingdom for the first time in the historiographic tradition of China. It is from the *Book of Han* and by the name *"Wa"*, that any foreign nation is known to have any knowledge of the existence of Japan.

The Yayoi period saw the establishment of military forts, the beginning of tribal and inter-clan warfare and with it, social stratification that is evident from the different grave-sights. This stratification in the society, in a way has continued up-to modern times presenting Japan with a strictly segregated class structure. During this period, metal-work, wood-work and even sericulture received a major boost. It is evident that Sino-Japanese relations existed at that time. This era also saw the consolidation of various tribes and clans into "Kingdoms". The exact number of these kingdoms is debated but the Chinese book of *Wei Zhi* gives a debated number -- a hundred kingdoms. This text also states that the number of states gradually decreased as a single kingdom by the name *Yamatai* gained ascendance over the others. This history is however, debated by historians.

Whatever be the case, the consolidation of the "Yamatai" or Yamato reign continued and what is today known as Japan evolved out of the complicated Clan-politics that was dominant in the early centuries. While still the clans and tribes held practically all power in Japan, the Emperor and the imperial family remained the nominal rulers of Japan from about 250 CE till modern times, Emperor Akihito being the 125th emperor of Japan. This clan politics and chaos subsided to a certain extent since the 6th century AD, a period that is marked by the beginning of poetic and literary compositions and aptly named the "Asuka Enlightenment".

The emperor's first stable and well established government was set up in Nara from the year 710 CE onward. Nara was the new capital designed after the Chinese capital Chang'an. This new capital was designed to be the centre of political as well as religious activities and thus a great many Buddhist temples and Shinto shrines were built during this period. Buddhism a religion that appeared in Japan from China in and around the seventh century CE was gradually gaining popularity and temples were getting powerful. However, the capital had to be soon abandoned and after a few intermediate ones, was ultimately changed to Heian-kyo ("the abode of Peace")--the present day city of Kyoto where it remained for a thousand years till the Meiji Restoration when it was changed again to Tokyo. The changing of the capital from Nara to Heian-kyo (794 CE) ushered in the period known as the "Heian Period" which is an era of unprecedented peace in Japanese history.

Out of all other "periods" of Japanese history, the part we really need to focus on is the Heian period. Because it is this era that produced some of the greatest works of classical Japanese literature, including the Ogura Hyakunin Isshu and the Genji Monogatari. The politics of the Heian period shows a gradual decentralization of power. From holding absolute power in the Nara period, the emperor's position dwindled as the Fujiwara clan gained ascendancy mainly through intermarriage with the Imperial family. As things were more "Japanised", the influence that China formerly had over Japanese culture and life also reduced manifold. The introduction of the *Kana* syllabic characters into the Japanese writing system made the use of Chinese characters no more imperative for writing.

In this period, the seeds of the future militarized feudal administration was also laid. Higher taxation forced many farmers to sell of their land and become tenants to big land-owners who often employed *samurais* to protect their lands. In due course, the Samurais would seize all the power and become the actual rulers of Japan.

It is true that the emperor was the sovereign ruler of Japan. But he was helped by a structured bureaucracy that was in a way similar to that of China.

To say that the bureaucratic structure was complicated would be an understatement. At the top of all such political structures sat the emperor, appointing all the lower officers. The entire bureaucracy was divided into ranks which were considered extremely important for a Japanese person. Most aristocratic men were addressed by their titles rather than their names. Women were addressed by the titles of a close relative and thus the title and rank formed an important part of their identities. The entire multitude of titles were divided up into nine ranks; the lowest of them being the ninth. The men holding the titles of the three highest ranks were designated as court nobles and were members of the 'Council of State'. The fourth and fifth rank-holders were regarded as 'senior courtiers' and the were granted access to the Emperor's quarters. This access was also granted to the Chamberlain (*kurodo*) (a post of the sixth rank) who, by duty had to attend to the emperor. The ranks below sixth were hardly significant in the hierarchical structure and these ranks were often associated with birth status. However, as appointment to offices was associated with rank, promotion was not an uncommon thing.

Another aspect of these titles was the division into "Left" and "Right" of the court nobles. This is a system derived from the Chinese bureaucratic style. Those sitting to the left of the emperor (i.e. The East side) were designated as "ministers of the left" and those sitting to the west, were "minister of the right" while the emperor sat facing the south. The ministers of the left had greater prestige in the court than the ministers of the right and the appointment to the left was seen as an event demanding a lot of celebration.

The Fujiwara ascendancy that began at the dawn of this age reached a peak during the times of Michinaga gradually began to decline. This was intensified by Emperor Go-Sanjo's strong antipathy towards the Fujiwaras and his attempts to rule without any sort of political constrains to his sovereignty. But the decline of the old bureaucracy also meant the weakening of the imperial government. This weakening is evident from the large number of feuds and disturbances that start from this time onward.

The two new clans that gained strength in the 12th century were the Taira (or Heike) and the Minamoto (or Genji). By this time the Taira had replaced several Fujiwara court nobles and the Minamoto had gained military ascendancy in the North following the wars between 1050 and 1087. After a series of battles and minor disturbances or struggles to assume power, known as the Heiji Uprising of 1159, Taira no Kiyomori appeared on the scene as the new leader of Japan. The little peace that Kiyomori's reign (through the Emperor), witnessed during the ten years of his rule till 1178 was again disturbed by the ensuing power-struggle between the two clans succeeded by the Genpei War (1180-85) and the subsequent rise of the Minamoto clan. After dispelling all challenges and opponents which even included his own clan-members, Minamoto no Yoritomo emerged as the supreme military leader of Japan and was appointed *"Shogun"* whereby he established the new government of Japan known as the Shogunate ruling from his home city of Kamakura and in the process reducing the Emperor to the status of a mere titular head which he remained for another six hundred years.

The cultural implications of this change is in reality incalculable. The peaceful days of the Heian period were over and the militarization of Japan had began. Soon a society would emerge where the Samurai(s) would be at the centre of attention and the real rulers of Japan. A prolonged period of chaos would continue till the subduing of all rival forces by Tokugawa Iyeasu in 1603. Thus the old ways of the society soon change to accommodate the new military mentality, the Kamakura period onward. This change often looked upon as a sad one points supports the gloom and sadness that hangs over the poems in the latter part of the anthology. With the rise of the new order in society, the new ideals such as those encoded in the *Bushido* and *Zen* Buddhist appeared on the scene which replaced the older forms of religion and code of conduct. All these changes are in reality apparent at the sub-textual level through the poems of the Hyakunin Isshu as we shall discuss.

Poets and Poetry in Japan

Japan is said to be the only nation, where the head of state viz. The Emperor regularly and religiously took part in the act of poetry composition. As mentioned before, poetry was not a mere leisurely activity in Japan. It was a more religious and a more transcendental approach to understanding the self. Thus, one of the principal duties of the king, required him to assume an active role in the composition of poetry. Thus, for a long time, poetry remained a strictly court-activity--a means of enjoyment of the elite. But it soon transcended the boundaries of class and pervaded the minds of even the humblest citizens.

In this regard, Buddhism played an active role. Buddhist monks are often found composing poetry and taking part in poetry-competitions. This was also a spiritual exercise for them. This concept also draws heavily from Chinese influences where writing was considered a 'spiritual exercise.'

Likewise, in Japan too, poetry first emerged in religions literature.

In fact the first poem is said to be not written by any mortal man but heavenly deities. The story is as follows:

The two first kami(s), Izanami and Izanagi roamed around the World Pillar and encountered each other when the first goddess, Izanami spoke first saying the following words:

> *What great joy it is,*
> *To see a man so fair.*

Being enraged at the female goddess' breach of etiquette and speaking first, the male god Izanagi asked her to depart and return later. When they reunited, Izanagi said:

> *What great joy it is,*
> *To see a woman so fair.*

This is the first instance of Japanese poetry are found in the Shinto bible--the Kojiki (712 CE). But, as rightly pointed out by the scholar Arthur Waley, those poems rarely portray the true genius of Japanese poetry. They are too much weighed down by the weight of the contexts that they are speaking about and thus is very close to "poetic prose" rather that beautiful poetry. Here, it is important to mention that Japanese poetry almost never had any tradition of using rhyming words. Rhyme was seldom used and that too was for a specific purpose. Development of poetry in Japanese has always focused on the content rather than the tone. Another important aspect of Japanese poetry is the use of measured syllables. The Japanese poets developed several forms of poetry with greater focus on the syllable count of each line than the content. In this way *tanka, haiku, hokku, haikai* etc. developed as forms of short poems. The Man'yoshu which is again the oldest poetry collection of Japan contains a substantial number of long poems or *choka(s)* but they also follow the standard format of alternate lines with five and seven syllables each. These *choka(s)* tended to become very long, dragging and tiresome to read and violated the Japanese principle of minimalism thereby destroying the beauty of poetry. Probably because of all these reasons the poets decided to abandon this form and stick to the shorter forms of poetry; principally the *tanka*--a hundred of which will be found in the Ogura Hyakunin Isshu.

As discussed before, the word "tanka" literally means "short song". It typically must contain thirty-one syllables and five lines. The 31 syllables are broken into the five lines following the 5-7-5-7-7 pattern. They are usually personal responses to a certain natural or emotional phenomenon or a beautiful sight. Ideally, a *tanka* or even the more popular *haiku* (5-7-5) must consist of two parts that may or may not be separated by a gap in between (usually haikus are not). These two parts should have a stark difference in the approach to appreciation of the same object or phenomenon. This is what is known as the *kiri* or cutting effect in a *tanka* or a *haiku*. Tankas originated roughly during the period known, in Japanese history, as the Asuka enlightenment--sometime in and around the 7th century CE. They found their place among the tales in the Kojiki and Nihon Shoki and ultimately came into the folds of the Man'yoshu and later imperial anthologies such as the Kokin Waka-shu, the Gosen Waka-shu, the Shuishu, the Shika Waka-shu etc.

Here, I believe it is imperative to reiterate the fact that the term *"waka"* refers to poetry written in the Japanese language and not to any particular form of it. However, the most dominant form of poetry in the Imperial anthologies was the *tanka* and thus it came to be almost equated with the term *waka* however, it is not wrong to call a *haiku* a waka as well.

Haiku(s) emerges a little later, probably in and around the fifteenth century and found in Matsuo Basho, a champion of haiku composition. Haiku(s) are however different from Tankas. Haiku(s) being very short do not contain personal responses to the natural scene being recorded but act as a mere transmitter of the beauty of it from the eyes of the poet to the mind of the reader. This is again an influence of the uniquely Japanese idea of 'minimalism.' The Japanese people believe that it is not important to reveal the emotions trapped in the poets mind, that the mere beauty of the composition is enough to affect the mind of the reader and move it with a similar experience. Here, it would be worthwhile to mention the story of the Haiku poet Chiyo:

Chiyo (1703 - 1775) was a female Haiku composer living in Kaga; she was already famous among her friends as a fine poet but desired more than just local fame. With this intention in mind, she called on a Haiku master visiting her town and desired to be trained by him. The master asked her to compose a Haiku on the subject "Hototogisu" or the Lesser Cuckoo. One prominent characteristic of this bird is that it sings while it flies at night and therefore also heralds dawn. Chiyo tried her best but her master rejected each and every haiku that she wrote as "merely conceptual". She did not know how to transmit her true feelings genuinely. One night she went on a deep search for the perfect haiku and did not notice that it was already dawning. The screens in her house were slowly lighting up when suddenly a haiku formed in her mind. She wrote:

Hototogisu,	Translated as:	Calling "cuckoo", "cuckoo",
Hototogisu tote,		All through the night,
Akenikeri.		It dawns at last.

Her master accepted it as the finest haiku on this topic as it truly communicated the author's own feelings.

Thus in the Japanese ideal, the poet is not supposed to be human when composing poetry. He is supposed to be merely an instrument through which the artistic instincts may be transmitted from the poet's eyes to the reader's mind. These ideas were expanded and evolved to become, what is known as the *Zen* Perspective of Art. The concept that all artistic instinct dwell far away from this mortal world and are unaffected by our activities, that it dwells in the realm of the *Zen* was instrumental in creating this idea about the artist being a mere translator and a transmitter of that artistic instinct from the Higher Realms to the Common Realms.

This whole idea of the artist being a transmitter of something dwelling in the Realm of the Zen became the main reason why so much importance came to be attached with artistic creations--why it became a spiritual exercise. And the Emperor of Japan being a *kami* himself and the protector of the Shinto faith, could not evade this practice either and thus extreme importance was given to the Emperor's role as a poet. The emperor, in the Heian period was actually seen to fulfill the role of a sage-king--a concept probably imported from China, whereby his duties included the propagation of not only religion but also the culture of the people and poetry formed an intimate part of Japanese culture in the Heian period. Thus the emperor is also found to actively support poetic activities by holding poetry-competitions, commissioning anthologies and the likes.

Here it should be mentioned that Poetry was a very serious business and a way of holding status in society among the nobility of the Heian period. Poetry was a subject included in the Civil Service (or Imperial) Examination of China and Japan. As poetry gained more and more importance with the aristocracy, it also became common among ordinary literate men to indulge in poetic compositions. The exchange of *Waka* became common among lovers and thus the poetic tradition received a further impetus. Poetry writing, reciting and compiling became everyday affairs. People also started to give a lot of importance to memorizing poems and waiting for the appropriate occasion to boast their poetic understanding. It is said that Emperor Murakami memorized over 1000 poems from the *Kokin Waka-shu*.

Chinese influences in the poetry of Heian period cannot be overlooked as well. As Japanese language and writing system draws heavily from China, so does their literary styles. In fact one of the major form of poetry found in Japan was the *Kanshi* -- the name given to Chinese poetry (literally Han-shi). Among the highly revered Chinese classics was Bo Juyi's "Song of Unending Sadness" (*Cheng-hen-ge*). The affair between the Emperor and a concubine as described in the poem, served as a major source of inspiration for many poetic works including one in the Ogura Hyakunin Isshu. It is thought to be an important source of inspiration even for Murasaki Shikibu in framing the character of Prince Genji.

With the ensuring Hogen Rebellion and other disturbances, the Heian period drifted into what is known as the Kamakura period. Characterized by the downfall of the central authority in Japan and a decline in the status of the Emperor, the Kamakura period onward heavy militarization is seen in Japan. The '*Shogun*' took over the reins of administration and entered into severe conflict with the surrounding warlords and leaders. This period saw a slight decline in the poetic tradition as frequent insurrections disturbed the peace of the nation. However, it produced the most important man in the Ogura Hyakunin Isshu--the compiler, Fujiwara no Teika. He is credited for having created the three schools of *waka* -- the Nijo, Reizei and the Kyogoku family styles (passed on by his three descendants) which marks a turning point in the cultural history of the Kamakura period.

The later periods of Japanese history are considered irrelevant for understanding the current text and thus are left out from this Introduction.

Turning to society, Japanese society has since the ancient times been very strict and rigid. Marked by extreme stratification Japanese society presented an ideal view of a society where social status, primarily ascribed was derived from birth and not by merit. But the noblemen born into the noble households were expected to gain certain qualities through their lives and one of them was the ability to compose poetic verses. This was more of a social obligation in the part of the aristocrats to patronize poets with talent than it was a choice. Under these circumstances, the poetic tradition of Japan is bound to get enough impetus to flourish in the Heian period.

Finally, the poets of Japan came from all levels of society. As poetry became more and more a means of communication between lovers and the likes, poetic tradition pervaded all class barriers and touched the level of even the humblest men. Poets coming from all ranks came to be greatly revered and they almost formed a class by themselves. Poets often came from Buddhist and Shinto religious backgrounds and were often related with the Chinese concept of Sages. In fact the early poets of the Hyakunin Isshu like Hitomaro were in fact equated with the idea of sages. And it is from there that the Thirty-Six Poetry Immortals and the Six Poetic Sages etc. developed.

A Note on Translation

To say, that the poems of the Hyakunin Isshu have been translated into English in this book would be a grossly mistaken statement. I prefer to claim that I have rendered them in the English language for the common English reader not very different from myself. My translation is very liberal for I have tried to preserve the poetic essence of the verses. Due to the huge cultural gap between Japan and England, there exist a great variety of Japanese words and phrases which cannot be literally translated to English. Thus I present quatrains portraying the thoughts and the imagery of the poem in the best possible way that is closest to the original Japanese. In doing so, I have compared the current version with former English translations of those verses by William N. Porter in his book *"A Hundred Verses from Old Japan"*, Professor Joshua S. Mostow from his book *"Pictures of the Heart: The Hyakunin Isshu in Word and Image"* and Clay McCauley.

The English verses presented here, are not always in a regular rhyme scheme, mostly quatrains though five-line poems are also there; and I think I should reiterate the point that these are **not** simple translations of the original poems and thus if a reader wishes to read the poems in original, retaining its true meaning, splendor and beauty, I sincerely advise him to read the original verses in Japanese because the pleasure derived thence is incomparable to that derived from any translation.

With all that said, we should now delve into the most popular anthology of Japanese verse, the Ogura Hyakunin Isshu. But before that, the poem written below demands explanation. It was written by Emperor Nintoku and is considered as the first poem that any poetry-student should learn. Moreover, it is religiously recited before a *Karuta* match involving the Hyakunin Isshu. Thus I felt it my duty to incorporate the text and translation of it before I officially begin the anthology. It speaks about Emperor Nintoku's return to the throne after an interregnum of a few years. The blooming of the flowers metaphorically refer to the restoration of the Emperor to the throne. *Sakuya* here refers to blossoms, particularly plum blossoms that bloom just before the cherry.

The first poem having been sung, the journey from Emperor Tenchi to Emperor Juntoku's times from a poetic niche has now begun. Being an anthology dating over many centuries, I have also made it a point that the historical background of the poems are not overlooked. This provides an ideal opportunity to re-evaluate history from a different angle and a novel, first-hand insight.

Emperor Nintoku

Naniwa-tsu ni,
Sakuya kono hana,
Fuyu go mori.

Ima wo haru be to,
Sakuya kono hana.

The flowers bloom again,
In Naniwa's Bay
Dormancy of winter,
Has now passed away,
In the reign of the Spring,
The flowers bloom again.

-- Kokin Waka-shu

The Ogura Hyakunin Isshu

(A Hundred Poems by a Hundred Poets)

1

The Autumn Harvest Hut

Emperor Tenchi

Aki no ta no,
Kari ho no io no,
Toma o arami,

Waga koromode wa,
Tsuyu ni nure tsutsu.

In this autumn field of rice,
I sit in this harvest hut
My sleeves have now been wet
By the moisture dripping through.

How wise for such an emperor whose deeds are now a legend to have composed such a poem, and then again one cannot miss marveling at the wisdom of the compiler to begin his anthology with this. But is the emperor really being drenched by the dripping autumn dew? Perhaps. This wetting of the sleeves may be with tears. This may be interpreted as a love poem as well but lacking substantial information, we choose otherwise.

During Emperor Tenchi's reign of ten years, from 661 to 671 CE, the 'Taika Reforms' were promulgated. Mainly a set of agricultural reforms, it enhanced the imperial authority in the sphere of agriculture. And perhaps it brought the peasants into close links with the emperor and the imperial household.

This poem though may be interpreted as a love poem because of its mention of wet sleeves, typical of love poems in Japan, Teika wanted it as the poem of a caring emperor. This emperor, Tenchi, knows the hardships of the people. He knows their pains and gains and thus, he knows that the empire is prospering. And it is that prosperity that, is dripping through the roof and wetting the emperor's as well as the farmer's sleeves who wait at the paddy-shack.

Here the emperor portrays himself as a farmer, waiting all through the night, at a harvest-hut.

The poem has another significance in this anthology: for it is the first poem. Other than chronological causes, Emperor Tenchi was the very person to bestow the honorific title "Fujiwara" upon Nakatomi no Kamatari and thus by beginning the anthology with this poem Fujiwara no Teika also tells the story of his clan.

2

The White Silk Robes

Empress Jito

Haru sugite,
Natsu ki ni kerashi,
Shirotae no,

Koro mo hosu cho,
Ama no Kaguyama.

The spring has now passed,
And the Summer breathes again,
While the silk robes are drying on
The Heavenly slopes of Kaguyama.

The Sun goddess, Amaterasu, is said to be the divine progenitor of the line of Japanese monarchs by virtue of which all Japanese emperors right from Emperor Jimmu till Emperor Weido (d. 1989) claimed divine status. It is said that Amaterasu has once closed a stone door on this Mount Kaguyama thereby depriving the world of her blessings as well as sunlight. In the poem it says, that 'white silk robes' are drying on that Heavenly Kaguyama. The white silk robes are probably the blessings that Amaterasu has bestowed upon the empress which is marked by the empire's prosperity during her reign.

The slopes of Kaguyama are now white--this means that the empress' parental peer, Amaterasu is happy at her reign and is showering blessings on her and the kingdom. In fact, Jito's reign (687 - 697 CE) is often referred to be 'full of light and brightness'. But this may also allude to the chaos of the former times, or the period when the world was plunged into darkness, that ultimately subsided with the stable reign of Tenchi and Jito and thus Kaguyama is all bright again.

As most Tanka and Haiku poems, this one too has a double interpretation. This may simply be understood to be a poem describing a natural scene as well. Mount Kagu (Kagu-yama) is one of the three Nara hills sung to by Emperor Tenchi in his famous *choka* and her daughter Jito could clearly see it from her palace--the Fujiwara no Miya. So, the white robes are drying may also simply mean that the mist enshrouding the mountain is now slowly clearing and the robes(veils) that hid the divine mount are vanishing slowly.

3

The Mountain Pheasant's Tail

Kakinomoto no Hitomaro

Ashibiki no
Yamadori no o no
Shidari o no,

Naganagashi yo no,
Hitori ka mo nen

Like the long dragging trail,
Of the mountain-pheasant's tail--
How long must I lie alone
Through this long, eternal night?

With this poem, we enter into the world of the common poets. Hitomaro served in the royal court from about 680 CE (traditional date: Temmu 9), all the way till death in 710 CE. He witnessed the entire reign of Empress Jito which is said to have played a very important part in shaping him and fostering his poetic abilities. This poem has two aspects, one, the mountain pheasant's tail and the second, the poet lying alone, tied into one single expression of longing.

"Yama-dori" or 'Mountain Pheasant' is a bird found in the hilly tracts of Japan, popularly known as the "copper pheasant" it possesses a long and beautiful tail that drooping down, touches the ground and is dragged when it moves about. This dragging naturally leaves a long trail on the ground through the places that it has moved. This, the poet uses to describe his condition, which to him is like being dragged along the path of life. Or maybe, the night. He says, "the long, eternal night."("*Naganagashi yo no*") In a word, he feels lonely being left alone.

Again, in Japanese folk tales, the mountain pheasant is given a curious attribute. They are said to sleep alone at night when the pairs separate and sleep of opposite slopes of the mountains. Thus, the poet uses this to describe his own state as well and to allude to the absence of his wife(s) (possibly) both of whom are said to have died before the poet.

Hitomaro was often called, "the poet of sounds". It seems that this epithet was very true. If one recites the Japanese poem aloud, one will surely notice the repeating sound "no" which is the main feature of this poem and almost gives a rhyming effect to it. But this can also be seen to refer to the boredom in life.

If one reads these three poems together, the first, the second, and this, one finds a curious link in the three. All of these are approximately from the same period and their sharing a commonality cannot be a mere co-incident. Peter McMillan, in his book "One Hundred Poets, One Poem Each", says that he believes, "the dampened sleeves of the emperor [Tenchi] and Hitomaro are being symbolically hung out to dry by the daughter empress [Jito], whose reign is depicted as being full of brightness and light." Their great poetic abilities and prosperous reigns are perhaps the reason why Hitomaro feels himself to be drooping under their weight.

4

The Wise Mount Fuji

Yamabe no Akahito

Tago no ura ni,
Uchi idete mireba,
Shirotae no,

Fuji no takane ni,
Yuki wa furi tsutsu.

Mount Fuji's peak I see,
White with drifting snow
Every time I take the path,
That leads to Tago's coast.

Should Mount Fuji not find a place in this famous anthology? After all, it surpasses all other Japanese mountains in fame. Yamabe no Akahito, referred to as the "poet of images", (like Hitomaro is called the "poet of sounds"), is perhaps the best person to accomplish the job. Here, the poet simply captures the sight of Mount Fuji with snow on its peak, as he sees it from Tago's coast.

But when commenting on this poem we have to remember that Mount Fuji is believed to be a God and it is not likely that the poet will speak lightly of it. Thus probably we need to find intricate details, more than what is evident from the poem. Upon searching, we find a *choka* (longer poem) in the Man'yoshu (compiled in about 759 CE) that for the first time mentions this legendary mountain in that anthology. The poem there starts by describing its mythical origin as recorded in the *"Kojiki"* and sings praise to the mountain. One certain line in that choka, deserves special mention and clarifies to the reader the deep veneration the people had for this mountain. It says:

> "Even the high clouds,
> Do fear to move above it."

----- Man'yoshu (3: 317 - 318)

This gives the sense that Mount Fuji is venerable and the special mention of snow at its peak may allude to the fact that Mount Fuji is referred to be old and wise and the white snow (like white hair) is the proof of its wisdom. Its age is also sung to in that *choka,* saying:

> "Since the heaven and earth were parted,
> It has stood, godlike....."

----- Man'yoshu (3: 317 - 318)

As an envoy to that *choka*, there is a shorter five line poem that almost matches the one found in the Ogura

Hyakunin Isshu except for a few word. The one in the Man'yoshu says:

"Tago no ura yu	Translated as:	Going out on Tago Bay
uchiidete mireba		when I look
mashiro ni so		it is pure white;
Fuji no takane ni		on the high peak of Fuji
Yuki wa furikeru"		snow is falling.

--- Man'yoshu (3: 318) Translated by Anne Commons

This fact matters, because we have an ongoing debate as to who Akihito was. And this proves that this poem might also be attributed to someone else and it is just one version of the text.

I wish to add another interesting fact to this commentary. If we take a look at a different and a more line-by-line translation of this poem, we see in action a very classical tanka-writing technique. If we look at the following translation by Clay McCauley,

When I take the path
To Tago's coast, I see
Perfect whiteness laid

On Mount Fuji's lofty peak
By the drift of falling snow.

(Source: University of Virginia, library)

We find that the first three lines, have no reference to the mountain. The whiteness that is mentioned might also be used to refer to the waves or the shore. But then suddenly from the coast, it turns to the lofty mountain. This juxtaposition, in a sense, is a typical feature of Tanka poems.

"Tago no ura" is presently the Suruga Bay in Shizouka prefecture of Japan.

5

The Wandering Stag

Sarumaru Dayu

Okuyama ni
Momiji fumiwake
Naku shika no,

Koe kiku toki zo,
Aki wa kanashiki.

Away on secret mountain tracts
The crimson leaves adorn the paths,
When I hear the Stag's cry: I know--
How sad the autumn is.

Truly, how sad the autumn is. When one knows that all the warmth of the world will bid adieu and the cold and frosty winter will set in! This poem depicts autumn. This is also the first poem to describe a season with many others to follow. Sarumaru Dayu or Sarumaru no Taifu has thus opened unto us the richest and most picturesque themes in Japanese poetry--Autumn. Autumn is associated with the colour crimson red and this shade predominates the palette, when it comes to the portrayal of the season

The leaves dry up and fall paving the ground, their rustling fall being the only sound in the woods. This image cluster forms the stock metaphor for autumn as we see in this poem. These familiar sights and sounds are enhanced here as now the sound also signifies the wandering lonely stag. The rustling sound is understood, though not mentioned, to be caused by the walking of the stag through the leaf-paved woods. And it is this sound that catches the attention of the poet. For the language makes it clear that this feeling of loneliness, as often, is a fleeting realization. Then the cry of the "lonely" stag reminds him of his own loneliness. The stag, mateless, treads the leaf laden path in search of her.

The poet seems to relate himself to this situation, however we cannot be sure because very little is known about Sarumaru. Some say that nobody of that name existed at all; and it was Prince Yamashiro no Oe who used the pseudo-name, Sarumaru Dayu.

Inspite of his own loneliness, the poet says "aki wa kanashiki" or "sad autumn" which is a general statement. So, he says that autumn itself is sad. This is quite common in several cultures of the world, particularly in countries like Japan where the winters are extremely harsh and often disrupt normal life. Here, the poet sees the leaves "aging" or turning yellow and then to red. Finally they will fall on the ground and clothe the world in red. The winter is approaching, death and dormancy of nature is coming and thus the poet is reminded of his mortality and isolated nature of the human soul which is all about eternally searching for its ideal mate. As all the warmth around him is gradually going out. So, here, autumn is the season for bidding goodbye to this warmth and love and generosity. Thus, the Autumn is a sad season; and so is the poet. The sadness of the autumn seems to resonate in his mind and bring back the feeling of abandonment--and thus loneliness. This is where we can aptly compare the feeling of "memento mori" or reminder of death with the feelings of this poet.

Here the stag bears special significance. A "lonely stag calls" definitely is an allegory to the sadness of the season. He uses this in the sense of the idiom "as swift as a stag." The call of the stag, is most likely the call of the season. When the poet hears this call he knows that it is time to bid goodbye to the mellow summer (as it is in Japan) and this knows that the autumn is lonely. But then he is reminded of the swiftness of the stag and also knows that this loneliness is momentary as the stag swiftly goes away in search of its separated partner.

6

The Bridge of Magpies

Otomo no Yakamochi

Kasasagi no,
Wataseru hashi ni,
Oku shimo no,

Shiroki o mireba,
Yo zo fuke ni keru.

That bridge of flying magpies,
Painted white with falling snow,
If I see across the sky;
The dawn is near, I will know.

This poem deserves to be explained in detail for it is a poem by one of the greatest poetic geniuses of this period Otomo no Yakamochi. Incidentally, Yakamochi is the very person thought to be the compiler of the Manyoshu i.e. the oldest and largest collection of Japanese poetry. This poem is symbolised by the "magpies"; the first line, being the decisive line. It can be interpreted in extremely diverse ways and perhaps is the most mysterious poem in the Hyakunin Isshu. First a general imaginary maybe taken into account.

The magpies are mainly dark-coloured birds. If they are seen to fly in great numbers across the sky, then the sky turns black. The poet uses this as an allegory of the night sky. When gently the white snow is falling over their wings, they are gradually turning into white birds and thus the night is turning into the day. But this interpretation is not accepted by the modern scholars but is enough to fire the imagination of a person and give an idea of the exact nature of these poems.

The other interpretations say that, the poem simply refers to a night scene in the Imperial Palace which were often adorned with short bridges. They say that when the poet uses the utamakura (epithet) "kasasagi" or magpie, the poet refers to a bridge in the Imperial Palace that he saw turning white due to the falling snow on a cold winter night. He uses the word "magpie" just to make it seem more poetic and fancy as well as to increase the weight of the term and perhaps to veil the true meaning.

Whatever it be, magpies find a prominent place in the cultures of the world. The ancient Romans considered them to possess great mental and intellectual powers, so they associated the bird with Baccus, the God of Wine.

However in the East, mainly China, the magpie is related to omens such as homecoming of family and friends, love as well as reunion. The cry of a magpie is said to herald the coming of a friend. Thus they are considered a good omen in China and probably Japan as well.

Magpies usually build their nest on the thickest V of a tree. These forks and V's in nature are symbols of gateways or paths into the spiritual realm. Thus these magpies guide us to the spiritual realm of the world and ask us to see deeper into life and our surroundings.

These two facts put together, we find another interpretation of this poem which is purely mythical in nature. It is based on the well known legend of Tanabata which relates how a group of magpies formed the bridge and helped *Orihime (the daughter of the King of the Skies)* to reach *Hikoboshi (the cow-herder star)* for one night when her enraged father had destroyed the only bridge lying over the River of Heaven.

The relation is surely evident now, the bridge of magpies here, is the bridge that the poet longs to see, that might bridge the gap between him and his partner. But in this case, the poem attains a sad note, because as per the legend of Tanabata after one night of union, there is going to be separation and waiting for another entire year. Perhaps his partner is dead, and thus he needs the bridge that will run "across the sky." But this explanation does not clarify the requirement of the frost. Which though maybe thought to be an analogy of the days that he is spending without his partner. So, considering the entire poem, perhaps the traditional interpretation would be more acceptable. Which says, that the poet simply describes the night turning into the day. The magpies are swooping down just before dawn and he thinks the sky is filled with black magpies, on which the nascent daylight is shining (like frost?) and the night is turning into the day.

7

The Memories of Home

Abe no Nakamaro

Ama no hara,
Furisake mireba,
Kasuga naru,

Mikasa no yama ni,
Ideshi tsuki kamo.

When I see the moon,
Walking the sky at night,
I ask myself if it is the same,
That rose on Mount Mikasa.
In the land of Kasuga.

At an early age, Nakamaro showed an inclination and a natural talent for mathematics. Coupled with his academic success, he quickly assumed the post of an official in the royal court. In 717 CE he was sent to T'ang China on a mission to learn the Chinese methods of time calculation. However, after the mission was completed, he tried several times to come back to Japan but failed each times, mostly because of shipwrecks. Thus he was compelled to stay in away from his home, in China, though most of his companions returned home, from 717 till his death in 755 CE.

This is a poem where he longs to be at home. From his home in the Nara court he must have seen the moon rise over Mount Mikasa (Mikasayama), that is the current Mount Wakakusa, located in the present Nara prefecture. Now, from the distant land, he sees the moon rise over an alien mountain or a plain and asks himself, "is this moon the same?" Maybe he could never accept the fact that he has to live here forever. So it is understood that this poem was written sometime between 717 and 755 AD which is, clearly in the most prosperous time of the Nara Period.

8

A Monk in Solitude

Kisen Hoshi

(Monk Kisen)

Waga io wa,
Minako o tatsumi
Shika zo sumu,

Yo o Ujiyama to,
Hito wa iu nari.

My lonely hut is here,
Away on Uji mount,
And it is so I choose to live,
Though the men all around,
Call it a "mount of Gloom."

This is a mysterious poem in the Hyakunin Isshu. As for the poet, we know almost nothing except that he lived in the early Heian period. He was a Buddhist monk and lived, as he says himself, on Mount Uji or Ujiyama. The reference to gloom and sorrow is what puzzles the readers in this particular poem. Mount Uji came to be known so, probably because of the Uji river. Now rivers are oft related with sorrow and tears so, the naming may have been hinted by Kisen in this poem, but this theory is debated. It is said, that Kisen himself took to Buddhism started living here out of grief and weariness of the world. And maybe through this poem he simply says--"I am content here." As it is a Buddhist practice right from the days of the Buddha to live in seclusion away from the frenzy of the world, Kisen might have chosen the Uji mountain as his retreat, being an unpopulated and solitary place, which was to the south-east of the capital, then at Kyoto.

However, we must also consider the possibility that the mount Uji had won the epithet "Mountain of gloom" or sorrow from Kisen himself who, as said before, went there a disturbed man and started living there. We come to this hypothesis for, since then the Ujiyama had been renamed after its resident as "Kisen-zan". The famous Buddhist temple, Byodoin, is also found there.

At this point the reader must take note of the fact that from this poem onward, leaving the Nara, we have entered into the Heian period.

9

Transient Beauty

Ono no Komachi

Hana no iro wa,
Utsuri ni keri na,
Itazura ni

Waga ni yo ni furu
Nagame seshi ma ni.

The flower's colour fades
As I watch the long rain
And wade through idle thoughts--
My life passes in vain.

Again we come back to a female poet. In our journey so far, we have read poems of one Emperor, an empress, a number of court nobles, a poetry genius and one solitary monk. Now here is a poem by a consort or a lady-in-waiting of no noble birth, probably to Emperor Nimyo (833-850). This poet, Ono no Komachi, was a lady of beauty past compare, so does legend claim and won the favor of many a courtier, many of them of a high rank such as Fukakusa no Shosho. But beauty fades with time. It is believed that this poem was written in old age.

The old age mentioned here, may not always be literal old-age though. Japanese waka often mentions a sort of old age, that is derived from a complex emotional feeling called "mono no aware" (pronounced: aa-wa-re). "Mono no Aware" does not have a direct English meaning, it may be translated as the "pathos for things" or basically pity for the transient nature of things. Pity for impermanence. Here, old age is used in that sense, the transience of life finds prominent mention in the fourth line.

An interesting point to note is the final line. Here she mentions the long drops of rain. In one sense these are literally raindrops. These are raindrops when we take the apparent meaning of the poem, that the raindrops are washing away the colours of the flowers, as time passes... and the flower is gradually drooping. But we all know that it is not possible. So we have to turn to the other meaning. Here the flower is her beauty that is fading away with time, like the wilting of a bloom. Here the raindrops are the tears and sweat that scar her face, used in the same sense that appears in the first poem, "my sleeves are getting wet/with the moisture dripping through." However, here the poet definitely pines for her beauty and her failing health instead of the kingdom or the people, perhaps this is a difference that we may expect to observe among the different classes that is, the difference between the thoughts of an emperor and a consort, in the case of such a stringent class-oriented society such as early Japan.

An alternative interpretation of this poem may also be considered. In another poem found in the *Kokin Waka-shu*, attributed to Ono no Komachi, (quoted below) she claims that the flower that wilts without any outward sign is the heart of man. Thus the *"Hana no iro"* or colour of the flower mentioned in this poem may well be the warmth in the heart's of men (i.e. her lover.)

Iro miyede	Translated as:	A thing which fades
Utsurou mono wa,		With no outward sign
Yo no naka no		Is the flower
Hito no kokoro no,		Of the heart's of men
Hana ni zo ri keru.		In this world.
		Courtesy: Arthur Waley.

10

Travelers On a Journey

Semimaru

Kore ya kono
Yuku mo kaeru mo
Wakarete wa

Shiru mo shiranu mo
Osaka no seki.

Travelers come and go,
Treading different paths.
But this is where, they all must meet,
At the gate of "Meeting Hill".

Traveling received a boost in the Heian-Period as the chaos and conflict subsided and highway-patterned roads started to be built connecting major destinations. This poem refers to "Osaka no seki" or the Osaka Barrier (In no way is it related the modern city of Osaka.) which forms the barrier between Yamashiro and the then capital Heian-kyo (currently, Kyoto) in the present Shiga Prefecture. It controlled the road to the capital and all the people from various parts of the country traveling to the Heian-kyo had to pass the gateway. Moreover the travel roads to Eastern Japan began from this Osaka Barrier making it a very important thoroughfare for daily travelers to the capital as well as those who undertook a journey for some particular purpose once in a while.

This poem may, however be interpreted in a different light as well. 'Travelers' may refer travelers through life and and this poem may mean that all men whether strangers or friends ("*Shiru mo shiranu mo*") must come as one to the gate of Osaka, which is also the gateway to the Imperial capital, the emperor's residence after death for the final judgment which is the task of *King Enma* (the ruler of the underworld). But since, in the Chinese and Japanese scheme of things, the emperor and the Gods were considered to be on the same plane of existence, this job might also be attributed to the emperor. After all, in those days, the emperor did have absolute authority over life and death.

11

Banishment

Sangi Takamura

Wata no hara,
Yasoshima kakete,
Kogi idenu to,

Hito ni wa tsugeyo,
Ama no tsuri bune

I'll spend my days in Yasoshima,
Alone, Far across the Sea,
Will the fishing boats that harbour here,
Kindly, tell my world of Me?

Poet, scholar, philosopher and a potential politician, Ono no Takamura (given the post of *"sangi"*) was a genius of many a trade. Yet it was this one request, or perhaps order, to go to China as an ambassador that earned him the displeasure of the nobility and added a sad overtone to his life. This is a poem written before or while on his voyage to the Oki Island, where he was sentenced to banishment for denying to be a part of the 837 CE Embassy to T'ang China. Japanese ships were not built to endure the mayhem in the deeper seas beyond the Japanese archipelago. Moreover, these envoys often had to stay for more that ten years in China and some of them never returned to Japan; like Abe no Nakamaro, the poet of the seventh poem in this anthology. It clearly states that he is being taken away from his homeland, and that too to the cold, lonely north-facing island of Oki, and the general tone itself says that it is against his wishes.

There exists a poem composed by Ono no Takamura during his banishment in the Oki Islands included in the *Kokin Waka-shu*. The tanka is quoted below.

Omoiki ya,	Translated as:	Did I ever think
Hina no Wakere ni,		That decaying in the wilderness
Otoroete,		Of a barbarian land
Ama no mawa tagi		I should become a shore-hunter
Isari-sen to wa.		Tugging at the ropes of fishermen
		Courtesy: Arthur Waley

Takamura's plight on being exiled is very apparent from this poem.

12

Divine Maiden

Sojo Henjo
(Monk Henjo)

Ama tsu kaze,
Kumo no kayoiji,
Fuki toji yo

Otome no sugata,
Shibashi todomen.

Oh Let the winds now blow,
And close the gates of Heaven,
So a little while now I may see,
These deities in mortal form.

Henjo lived a life of severe ups-and-downs, and when speaking of him or his poetry, it is necessary to have an idea of the changes in social status that he went through during his lifetime. At first he began as a "Minamoto" (surplus offspring of the imperial family) though there is no record as to whether this title was ever bestowed upon him or not. Anyhow, he began his life as a courtier and later, appointed to the position of a 'Kurodo' a sort of chamberlain by Emperor Nimmyo. After the Emperor's death, out of grief, he became a Buddhist monk, in spite of actively remaining in court politics. Even as a monk his social status underwent changes and from a simple practitioner of the Way, he was elevated to the post of "head priest" or a kind of temple manager of the two temples of Gangyo-ji and Urin-in around Kyoto.

So, it will be well enough to assume that his contacts with the imperial family, and the nobles remained almost intact throughout his life. What changed was the way he viewed Life itself.

This is definitely a scene from an imperial household where Henjo was invited to attend '*Gosechi*', a harvest festival of the eleventh month. Henjo's messengers in the waka could very well be the noble maidens who danced during the festival. It is believed that this dance form originated with Emperor Temmu's legendary visit to Mount Yoshino, as mentioned in the *Kojiki*. When night fell the emperor's *koto* had summoned the heavenly dancers unto earth. Here, Henjo is praying to the winds to shut the cloud gates so that these 'divine' maiden 'messengers' may be detained even if for a short while, from vanishing into the sky.

But if we slightly deviate from this simple explanation, and turn to the question why Henjo claims the maidens to be from the sky, we might have to seek assistance in Chinese thought. According to the Chinese view of the imperial hierarchy, nobility and divinity existed on the same continuum. The emperor's palace was believed to be in heaven and thus, the allusion may refer to this view as well, to say that the poet wants to delay the dancers from vanishing back into the folds of the inner palace. Implicitly it elevates the reign of Emperor Nimmyo to that of the great Temmu (Temmu was the 40th emperor and commissioned the building of the first capital city Fujiwara-kyo.) In which case, the poet may be said to be eulogizing to the emperor's reign.

13

Deep and Silent Love

Emperor Yozei

Tsukuba ne no
Mine yori otsuru
Mina no gawa

Koi zo tsumorite
Fuchi to nari nuru

That is how my love has grown,
Deep and silent still.
Like the River Mina's flow,
That rise from Tsubaka Hill.

More or less a simple poem, what needs explanation is the imagery here. Mount Tsubaka(4352 m) is one of the double peaked mountains of Japan located in the Ibaraki Prefecture. The two peaks of this mountain are from ancient times considered to be a man and a woman. In fact the name of the river Minano which rises from this Tsubaka Mountain is written in Kanji using the characters for man and woman. Anyways, scholars opine that this poem is addressed to Princess *Tsuridono no Miko* whom the emperor loved. The word *nuru* though may be an auxilary word for the word *nari (existence)* can also mean 'to wet' or to dampen. Thus, the poet probably says that he is being wet by his love for her and this is, in a way dampening him. *Koi* is a word to mean dark colour which used here, refers to the depth of the river Minano which compares the poet's love. But it may also mean love and must be understood to mean both.

In a word, he wishes to say that his love has grown very deep and strong (and perhaps torrential like a plunging river) and is comparable to the depths of the Minano river that plunges from Mount Tsubaka's peaks which resemble a man and a woman.

14

Disordered Prints.

Minamoto no Toru

Michinoku no
Shinobu moji-zuri
Tare yue ni

Midare some ni shi
Ware naranaku ni
Like disordered Shinobu prints
They dye in Michinoku,
I am held, confused now
And this is because of you.

At Michinoku, in the Province of Iwashiro, in old times a sort of figured fabric used to be made called *Moji-zuri* they were intricately designed using dye. The designing was done by placing vine leaves in between the cloths and rubbing or beating them with a stone until an impression was left on them. Shinobu grass is a type of fern used for this purpose and and thus it is referred to in this poem. However, "shinobu" also means "vine", "to love" or "to conceal" it may thus be correct to say that the poet wants to hint to his love as well using this word.

This poem is thought to be Toru's complaint of his wife or lover's faithlessness. He uses this beautiful imagery to convey how hurt he is when his wife is doubtful of his faithfulness. However, thus poem may also be interpreted as a confession of secret love to someone else, though that theory is debated.

It may be interesting to note that Michonoku is the older name of the present city of Fukushima in Fukushima Prefecture. *Moji-zuri* is also a plant possessing inflorescence flowers of purple colour that appear to twine around the plant itself. In modern Japanese, it is called, "Nejibana."

15

The Herbs of Spring

Emperor Koko

Kimi ga tame
Haru no no ni idete
Wakana tsumu

Waga koromode ni
Yuki wa furi tsutsu

It is as you bid,
That I pick green herbs in Spring,
Though my sleeves are painted white,
By the brush of falling snow.

It is generally believed that Emperor Koko composed this poem at an early age and that it refers to his picking some wild flowers and medicinal herbs (*wakana*) on New Year's day and sending them to someone. We are yet to identify the recipient of the herbs but this tradition continues in Japan. Even today, People eat green herbs after new year. This poem was sent as a gift to that unknown person along with some wild flowers and herbs.

Speaking of *wakana* we might assume that perhaps the recipient is ill or maybe dying. For wakana is a medicinal herb (like the Seven Herbs of Spring eaten after New Year) that drive away illnesses and bestows longevity. So, the recipient might be in dire need of these herbs and thus the poet says "it is as you bid" and then those gifts might have not been mere gifts at all but something much more important.

As to the explanation of the falling snow, we must know that the Japanese New Year in those days being celebrated according to the Lunar calendar, fell on various dates sometimes in late winter, sometimes in early spring. This means that in that particular year, the New Year fell sometime in late winter and that snowfall was still continuing at that time. But they might be used to refer to the emperor's condition seeing that person ailing as well which made him feel the Spring like the frosty winter.

16

The Sound of Pines

Ariwara no Yukihira

Tachi wakare
Inaba no yama no
Mine ni oru

Matsu to shi kikaba
Ima kaeri kon

I will, without fail,
Come back to you again.
If I hear the sound of pines
That grow on Inaba's peak.

A t first reading, this poem confuses the readers. How can the Pine trees make sounds? This is perhaps the perfect example of word-play in Tanka poems used to either mystify or hide its true meaning. The exact specifications of the poem, to whom it was written etc. Though remain unknown it is clearly to some lover whom Yukihira had forsaken with this promise to return if he hears the sound of the pines. In this tanka, *"Matsu"* plays an important role which means both "pine tree" and "to wait." So, if we incorporate the latter meaning in the poem, the meaning is complete. But, it is important to retain the original word, without which the poem loses its imagery and the word *"oru"* which is the noun form of the verb "to grow" becomes meaningless. Again, if *"ina"* and *"ba"* are separated from the word *Inaba*, *"ina"* means "to go" and *"ba"* may stand for "if" or "even if". So, what the poem wants to say is, even if I am going away today, I will wait for a chance to return to you. But perhaps, that chance will never come. It is a powerful emotion. Waiting for someone or something, knowing that it or that person will never come and that waiting will be eternal. Yet, waiting for the sake of waiting.

According to some scholars however, this poem is the final words of Yukihira when setting out on his journey for Inaba Province which was assigned to him to govern. It lies in the current Tattori Prefecture and Yukihira indeed was the provincial administrator there for some time. Later, being caught in political intrigues, Yukuhira was exiled and this poem might also be his final words before leaving for his banishment.

17

The River Dyed in Red

Ariwara no Narihira

Chihayaburu
Kami yo mo kikazu
Tatsuta-gawa

Kara kurenai ni
Mizu kukuru to wa

Even divine Gods,
Who reigned o'er ancient realms,
Never heard or said:
"Tatsuta dyes her waters in,
The hue of autumn red."

This poem is perhaps the most famous of all the poems in this anthology and surely the most picturesque of them. But explaining this poems demands a story. The poet, Ariwara no Narihara was in love with a lady of noble birth, Fujiwara no Takaiko who later married the emperor and became *Nijo no Kisaki* (Empress of Nijo). It is said, that it was the empress who demanded this poem to be written on the screens of her Nijo Palace. But it is said that even after this separation, Narihara's love for Takaiko never waned and it is precisely this that is portrayed in this poem behind the veil of allegory.

The imagery of the poem still captivates the readers. The Tatsuta river flows through the Nara Prefecture and at that point of time was adorned with trees or perhaps a forest on either banks. In autumn, the leaves have all turned red and that red is reflected in the waters of the river which also appears red. Then a few leaves are floating on the river and the poet thinks that the trees and the leaves are dying the river in autumn red by imparting their colours to it. Behind this allegory, the poet hints to himself who is imbibed by his love for the empress.

This poem also has a double meaning. The word *"chihayaburu"* is a pillow word or *utamakura* modifying the word *"Kami"* or 'God'. The poet wants to take this scenery as well as his love to a divine level by saying that his love for the empress is unmatched even for the divine and awe-inspiring gods. Literally *"chihayaburu"* means a "thousand swift swords" but can be used to refer to anything as powerful as them like the all-powerful gods as well as his love.

However, we must take note, that the river Tatsuta derives its name from the Goddess of Autumn, *Tatsuta-hime* who is said to resemble a man in her actions. This poem also alludes to this by saying that even the Gods cannot imagine Tatsuta doing something so feminine as dying. But, then again, it may mean that she is doing this without informing the other gods and may allegorically again refer to the poet's secret love for the empress.

The River Dyed Red, Poem number
17, Ariwara no Narihira

The poet--Ariwara no Narihira

18

If I Visit in Dreams

Fujiwara no Toshiyuki

Sumi no e no
Kishi ni yoru nami
Yoru sae ya

Yume no kayoi ji
Hito me yoku ran

Unlike the crashing waves
That gather at Sumi's Bay;
Even along the path of dreams,
See you if I may,
I have to hide away.

In this poem, we get to witness a Jokotoba in action. A Jokotoba is a short preface or reference to some natural phenomenon (as in this case) which may have some allegorical connection with the context of the poem but that is not a necessity. In this poem, Toshiyuki complaints of the constant public attention that Heian officials received. Which made it difficult to maintain private affairs. This poem was probably written at a waka contest held in 953

CE when these problems began to surface. In that rigid aristocratic system, he feels that he cannot visit his lover even in dreams unlike the ocean waves that gather openly at Sumi's Bay (Osaka Bay.) For if the words spreads in around the Imperial Palace, in those days an embarrassing fact could have destroyed one's career completely and he fears this.

In this poem, we also find a clever use of the word "*yoru*" (literally: "to approach: referring to, in the first case, the waves that approach Sumi's Bay and in the third line, mean "night". These two words though are pronounced similarly, are written differently in Kan-ji.

I would like to mention here, that *sumi* is also the noun for Japanese ink so, this poem can also be read as "Unlike the crashing waves/ that gather at the dark Bay."

19

Eternal Separation

Lady Ise

Naniwa gata
Mijikaki ashi no
Fushi no ma mo

Awade kono yo o
Sugushite yo to ya

Each other, we must never see,
Even for a moment,
As short as the reeds of Naniwa,
Is it what you want from me?

Lady Ise is another of the twenty-one female poets to find place in this anthology. This poem, though is fairly simple and straightforward deserves a little explanation. Scholars are of the opinion that Lady Ise wrote this either on being rejected and forsaken by a cold lover or perhaps this is a way to describe her plight at not being able to express her secret love for someone. We must admire the almost-rhyming word usage in this poem which drove me to translate it in a similar manner. In the Japanese original, the first and the last lines rhyme, both ending with the sound "ā". Again the second, third and fourth lines all rhyme with each other ending in "o".

'Naniwa Bay' or 'Naniwa Marsh' is another name of the now famous Osaka Bay. At that point of time, Osaka being a much smaller town was dissected by a a large number of streams and channels of running water which may have turned the place marshy. In Heian poetry, it is often associated with reeds and that too short reeds. Naniwa Bay finds prominent mention all through this anthology; reference to it is also found in the succeeding poem and poem numbered 88.

20

The Only Chance

Prince Motoyoshi

Wabi nureba
Ima hata onaji
Naniwa naru

Mi o tsukushite mo
Awan to zo omou

At Naniwa Bay we now must meet,
Even if I lose my life,
Miserable as it is now,
Those water-markers, I crave to see.

Prince Motoyoshi was the heir to the mad Emperor Yozei whom we encountered in the thirteenth poem of this anthology. As we read we can get a glimpse of how we are moving through time, first emperor Tenchi of the seventh century, then his daughter and now we find Emperor Yozei's son and we have already entered the early tenth century. We have flown across three hundred years in this short while from the first to the twentieth poem.

Prince Motoyoshi is said to have been in love with one of the hand-maidens of the retired Emperor Uda. But this maiden was favored by the emperor and had given birth to three of his sons. Moreover, she was the daughter of the extremely influential Fujiwara no Tokihira who even managed to convince the emperor to exile his favorite advisor, Sugawara no Michizane. The poet wants to say that even if it costs my reputation, I want to see that maiden whom I love. This is a bold expression indeed, considering the consequences if he was caught which was very probable as we know the public scrutiny problem as Fujiwara no Toshiyuki says (poem 18).

Here, the fourth line is crucial, if read as *"miotsukushi temo"* (身をつくしても) it means the famous water-markings or channel-barriers that mark the border of seas and channels. But otherwise, if read as *"mi o tsukishute mo"* (身を尽くしても) it means "even if my life I lose." The poet actually uses this to cleverly mean both of these and refer to his desperation to meet his lover.

21

The Broken Promise

Monk Sosei

Ima kon to
Iishi bakari ni
Nagatsuki no

Ariake no tsuki o
Machi izuru kana

I've waited for her because she said
"In a moment I will come";
I've waited months till the morning moon
Has appeared in the autumn sky.

There is a debate among interpreters whether this should be translated as "the autumn moon has risen" or whether it should mean "the morning moon has appeared", I tend to satisfy both the sides and thus translate this poem as it deserves to be. Again, some scholars feel that Sosei wanted to say that he has waited for an entire night but he clearly writes *"nagatsuki"* meaning "long month" so I feel that he wants to say that he has waited for a long long time which was utterly dark to him like the darkest night or perhaps that he has waited for an entire night which seemed to him an entire month. Anyways, since the latter interpretation explains the presence of the Moon, I accept it and leave it to the reader to decide which is more suitable to him or her. A striking feature of this poem is that the nature of the poet and the subject of the poem are not compatible. Sosei (the son of Henjo of the eighth poem) was a Buddhist monk, a man who is supposed to leave the world and live alone in seclusion away from petty matters. Then why does he say that he has waited for, probably his lover? Well, this is the nature of Tanka-poems to imagine oneself in another's condition and write a poem that way. Here, Sosei imagines himself to be an ardent lover waiting for his lady to come depending upon a parting promise she made. But she doesn't come. The promise is broken.

So, this should not take this poem as an autobiographical account lamenting his own condition. What is interesting in this poem is the admixture of various imagery into one single stream of expression. Here we see the morning moon, that symbolizes coldness and haziness. Then there is autumn--which itself brings the feelings of mourning, and heralds the cold, frosty weather.

So, in this poem the the poet feels that the night is passed and the morning moon has risen but then he is reminded that it is still autumn and the frost and coldness will soon draw in.

22

The Destroyer

Fun'ya no Yasuhide

Fuku kara ni
Aki no kusaki no
Shiorureba

Mube yama kaze o
Arashi to iuran

Autumn's leaves and grass are blown
And wasted by its breath.
Thus this wildest mountain wind
Is called-- The Destroyer.

An absolute genius of word-play we may call Yasuhide. In fact he is one of the Six Poetic Geniuses as selected by the compiler of the Kokin Waka-shu. In this poem he plays with the words *yamakaze* (山風) and *arashi*(嵐). "Yamakaze" means 'mountain wind' and "arashi" means 'storm.' But when written, employing Chinese characters in a top-to-bottom manner they can rarely be distinguished. So here, by the word mountain wind, he means storm so why did he need "arashi" again in the fifth line? There is the second word-play. He is punning the words "arashi"(storm) with the noun form of the verb *"arasu"* (to destroy). Here, we get to see a typical Chinese court poetry styled tanka which gives witness to the profound intellectual and poetic influence that China had over Heian Japan.

However, Fujiwara no Teika, requiring a more gentle and emotional poem in his anthology might have read it as a simple description of the desolation, and loneliness that the poet feels seeing the wind-swept landscape of autumn. It is best to read it thus and enjoy the beauty of the imagery.

23

The Autumn Guest

Oe no Chisato

Tsuki mireba
Chiji ni mono koso
Kanashi kere

Waga mi hitotsu no
Aki ni wa aranedo

With a clouded mind, I gaze at the Moon,
My thoughts are sad, but I believe
It is not my home alone
That Autumn is stopping by.

This poem follows the previous one in style. Here as well, we find the same punning of words and double-usage; giving it an array of meanings. This poem reminds us that we are merely a part of the world and definitely a part of nature. The moon inspires several deep thoughts in us. As it is autumn, naturally a feeling of isolation, loneliness, and a feeling of being forsaken binds the poet, but then again he sees the shining moon. In Japan, the 15th day of the 8th lunar month is celebrated as *o-tsukimi* or moon-viewing time.

The poet sees, the moon, perhaps remembers his past, and is sad. But then he is reminded that autumn has not only brought sadness and desolation to him and that the moon does not only shine for him--but the entire world. Perhaps a lighter thought.

24

The Leaves of Mount Tamuke

Sugawara no Michizane

Kono tabi wa
Nusa mo toriaezu
Tamukeyama

Momiji no nishiki
Kami no mani mani

A tribute to the Gods,
Are the brocade of red-leaves
Adorning Mt. Tamuke,
See them, for as of now,
I've come without an offering.

This poem is historical in nature. Accompanying his patron emperor Uda on an excursion, his loyal adviser Michizane failed to bring some offerings to the Gods wishing a safe trip. This was the prevalent custom of the day. In the poem, *"Nusa"* means "specific things" referring to the offerings that are dedicated to the gods as per Shinto rituals.

Just when he began to feel disheartened, he saw the brilliant sight of Mt. Tamuke adorned with crimson leaves that looked like a brocade decorating the mountain. Michizane, inspired by this scene decided to dedicate this brocade of red leaves that he discovered on Mount Tamuke to the Gods and in return wished for a safe excursion. Here again the dominant theme is Autumn, but for a change, this poem admires the beauty of autumn instead of relating it to sadness and isolation.

25

A Desperate Request

Fujiwara no Sadakata

Na ni shi owaba
Osakayama no
Sanekazura

Hito ni shirarede
Kuru yoshi mo gana

If your name is true,
Oh! Vine of "Meeting Hill",
Can you pull her by my side,
Away from other's eyes?

This poem was possibly composed to be sent to Sadakata's lover in secret. In those days, men and women often lived apart even in the imperial household. And if they were to meet, it was the man's duty to go and meet his lover or wife. In this poem, Sadakata puns the word "Osakayama" which means "meeting hill." He desires that the vines of meeting hill should pull his lover to him, if its name (meeting hill-- place of union) be true. Being against the custom, this has to be done in secret and so it is necessary that nobody should see it. Though he says *"osakayama no sanekazura"* whence we say "vine of meeting hill", (*'Sanekazura'* is a special type of climbing plant similar to wine-grass) the poet plays with this word as well. Sanekazura has *"sa"*, *"ne"* which may be translated as *"come"*, *"sleep."* and the final *"Kuru"* may as well mean "to come" or "to reel in." It is yet another *Kakekotoba*.

26

Oh! Autumn Leaves

Fujiwara no Tadahira

Ogurayama,
Mine no mojijiba,
Kokoro araba,

Ima hitotabi no,
Miyuki matanan.

Oh! Autumn leaves of Ogura,
If you have a heart,
You must halt, and wait
For the next royal pilgrimage.

This poem as well is historical in nature. This was probably written during or after an excursion along with the Imperial family to the banks of River Oi on Mount Ogura(Ogura-yama). The Emperor Uda, being moved by the sight of the maple leaves that had turned crimson red in autumn commented that his son (the future Emperor Daigo) should also visit the place. This led Tadahira, the emperor's faithful counsel to write this poem. In this tanka, he prays to those autumn leaves, growing on Mount Ogura to stop and delay their fall, stop their waning and halt till the next emperor should come and enjoy this delightful sight. Though he praises the beauty of autumn, the poet is reminded that this beauty is short-lived and merely a transient spectre.

27

Have we met before?

Fujiwara no Kanesuke

Mika no hara,
Wakite nagaruru,
Izumi-gawa,

Itsu-mi kikote ka,
Koishi karuran.

Like Izumi's stream
Wells-up in spate and flows,
Through the rocky crags.
I wonder, if we have ever met,
That I should pine for her.

Here again, the poet employs the typical Heian figure of speech--Jokotoba. The first three lines of the poem are a preface to the actual thought. A Jokotoba has a special feature that distinguishes it from an ordinary simile or analogy. That is, a Jokotoba may or may not have a direct relation with what is being said in the poem. The analogy may not be meaningful. It is understandable, for when a poet is writing during a poetry-competition he may not always have picturesque thoughts in mind. Even then, it might not be possible to put it into the prescribed 5-7-5-7-7 meter. It was during those situations, a Jokotoba came handy.

In this poem the Jokotoba does not bear a direct relation to the thought of the poem. The poet asks himself why does he pine for someone so much, when he is not sure if he has ever met her. But there is a little word-play here as well. Though "*Izumi-gawa*" means "river Izumi" referring to the actual river "Kizu-gawa", "izumi" can also mean a spring which wells-up and flows in spate through rocky crags. Which is both used to compare the sudden overflowing desire of the poet as well as to rhyme with the words "*itsu-mi*" *(when did I see)* in the fourth line. Professor Mostow, believes that, though unclear, in this poem Kanesuke may be sympathizing with lovers who have met once and cannot meet again. Perhaps the memory of that long ago meeting has almost died down, but suddenly, like a spring gushing through rocky cliffs, the desire to meet again conquers them.

28

The Loneliest of Seasons

Minamoto no Muneyuki

Yama-zato wa
Fuyu zo sabishisa
Masari keru

Hitome mo kusa mo
Karenu to omoeba

Troubled thoughts arise,
With withering leaves,
Departing guests,
Winter loneliness grows,
Along these mountain ways.

This poem, often deceives the readers. Minamoto no Muneyuki was not only a nobleman but the grandson of Emperor Koko. In those days, the Heian court officials were required to tour remote provinces at least once in every four years. Cut off from the royal court, away from the hustle of the capital was often a lonely affair for them. It is said that, he was away on such a trip when Muneyuki wrote this tanka that too as an answer to an old question. There was a debate among poets as well as courtiers whether autumn or winter was lonelier. Muneyuki certainly favoured winter. Through this poem he conveys his feeling of loneliness. The imagery is simple. The winter has set in, the grass of vines are blown away by the wind and the feeling of abandonment and desolation increases. The more lonely we are, the more we feel ourselves and perhaps that's the time when we realize how helpless our existence is.

29

The White Chrysanthemums

Oshikochi no Mitsune

Kokoroarte ni,
Orabaya oran,
Hatsushimo no,

Oki madowaseru,
Shiragiku no hana

Must it be that one,
The white chrysanthemum lying
Under the hazy frost,
Bewildered as in early fall,
That I might pick among them all?

This is a mysterious poem. It has been variously interpreted by the scholars of Japanese literature. Some say that it is merely an experimental poem using word-repetition. Other's claim rhetorical word-play. Some even doubt the mental condition of the poet. But this poem can truly be understood in more diverse ways than the ordinary ones. After all, Mitsune was one of the great poets and even among the thirty-six poetry immortals of Japan. I think two of the possible interpretations are most beautiful and poetic. One claims this poem to be an expression of timelessness. If the reader goes by the lines one would observe that it portrays the elements of the seasons in the reverse order. First, there is chrysanthemum, that is Spring. Then "hazy frost"-Winter. And finally it speaks of Autumn. And then, there is a choice. The poet says that he might pick that flower only by-chance--the white chrysanthemum lying abandoned in the hazy frost at the advent of autumn.

Another interpretation follows this assumption. Some believe that Mitsune might be speaking of wanting to resurrect a dead person and so he speaks of picking him from beyond the veils of time and thus the timelessness is spoken of.

The imagery is also captivating. The white chrysanthemum lying in the hazy frost. Some believe, that the words *"madowaseru"* meaning "to confuse", here actually refer to the poet being confused by the white chrysanthemum lying under the white snow which is camouflaging it. This may be an allegoric expression of the poet's love which has ended in a confusion and also may allude to his choosing his lover amongst a multitude of other ladies.

30

A Painful Parting

Mibu no Tadamine

Ariake no,
Tsuraneko mieshi
Wakare yori,

Akatsuki bakari
Uki mono wa nashi

Pitiless was my love,
Cold as the moon of dawn,
And now since we have parted,
What I dislike the most, is
The light of the nascent day.

It seems that the moon carried a lot of significance in romantic poems then. The time of the night when the moon is seen, the phase of the moon, all these bear a direct relation to the nature of the poem and the poet's emotions. Here the poet mentions *"Ariake"* which is a poetic term for the last rising moon of the last phase of the moon-cycle, thus is appears at that time when it is clearly discernable in the morning sky as well. Thus in many poems, the readers come across this term and it may be generally interpreted as the morning moon.

The morning moon, often fading and hazy may easily be equated with coldness and departure. From this poem, the reader can actually get a good idea of the tradition of Tanka poetry and where in the society it became a an indispensable practice. In Heian Japan, though men were allowed to keep a number of wives, it was not against moral law to dwell with a lover for one or two nights. Then after the day dawned, the men used to leave his lover's dwelling and return to their quarters. It was then a custom to write a short poem (usually Tanka) on a paper fan and send it to his lover through a servant. His lover used to reciprocate this gift by composing another poem in the same meter on a paper fan and sending it back with the servant. It was due to this custom that the number of love poems and particularly Tankas in Japanese literature is so immense.

This tanka was probably written for this very purpose by Tadamine to be sent to his lover after spending the night with her. That is why the poet mentions the morning moon which is cold because at the sight of it, he has to leave his lover, and deliberately uses the word "pitiless." The morning moon naturally detests the light of day, at the birth of which it must fade away. And he says that it is with equal hatred that he welcomes the new day; which heralds his departure from his lover's quarters. Truly cold indeed.

31

Drifting Snow

Sakanoue no Korenori

Asaborake,
Ariake no tsuki to,
Miru made ni,

Yoshino no sato ni,
Fureru shirayuki.

Like the light of the morning moon,
I saw at the break of day,
Under the haze of the drifting snow,
Yashino's village lay.

Again a reference to the morning moon *"ariake"*. Here the reference is clear. We can easily relate the coldness and whiteness of the scene to that of the morning moon. Here, the morning moon does not only portray emotional coldness but actual coldness as a sensation--but then again, the relation is imaginary. Yoshino village is probably the same Yoshino that lies in modern Nara Prefecture but scholars are not unanimous on this note. The term *"akatsuki"* used in the previous poem is a poetic term for "dawn" but here, the poet uses a very specific word, *"Asaborake"*--meaning "late dawn" usually refers to the dawn of late autumn and winter. Again, there is *"Ariake"*, a term found often in Japanese poetry and discussed thoroughly in the previous poem. Though in terms of language and imagery, it is similar to the previous one (Poem 30), in concept and expression it bears more similarity to the poem of white chrysanthemums (Poem 29).

Though Sakanoue no Korenori is one of the Thirty-Six Poetry Immortals of Japan, almost nothing is known of him. It is believed that he composed this poem while on a journey through these lands when he woke up and saw the Yoshino village under the "haze of drifting snow". The poet, wants to say that on this late dawn in winter, he could no longer discern whether the village was covered by snow or swept by gleaming moonlight. Lest the readers mistake it to be the light of the evening moon, he specifically mentions the morning moon thereby alluding to the coldness of the scene.

The similarity it bears with the twenty-ninth poem is evident. This is something that in Chinese poetry is called "elegant confusion." A sense of, not being able to discern one thing from another. This only shows the strong influence that Chinese literature had over Japan even in the late Heian period.

32

Strong, the Barrier Wall

Harumichi no Tsuraki

Yama kawa ni,
Kaze no kaketaru,
Shigarami wa,

Nagaremo aenu
Momiji narikeri.

Beyond this barrier wall,
The leaves of maple trees,
On the mountain-stream's flow,
Fail to fly away,
When the stormy winds blow.

This poem is fairly simple. Scholars are not yet sure why this poem was at all included in this special anthology. There is no word-play here, something that Fujiwara no Teika found very interesting; neither is there any picturesque imagery. What may have inspired Teika is the beautiful description of the Barrier that the wind has created (*"kaze no kaketaru shigarami wa"*) This poem simply describes a scene where the poet sees the maple leaves, torn by the stormy wind lashed upon the barrier upon the flowing mountain river. He feels that those leaves are trying to fly away but are powerless against the strong weir.

This may be read as a personal poem as well, where the poet feels himself thrown against that barrier which, in spite of trying hard, he cannot cross over. But for now, this remains a poem veiled in mystery as long as something more is not known about the poet himself.

33

The Spring that Goes By

Ki no Tomonori

Hisakata no,
Hikari no dokeki,
Haru no hi ni,

Shizu gokoro naku
Hana no chiruran

In the perfect days of Spring,
In the ever-shining light of Sun,
Why do the cherry, blown away
Scatter like streamless thoughts?

The poet speaks of himself or the Spring? It is not clear and this is verily one of the unique trends of Heian poetry also inspired by Chinese literature. Here the poet sees the advent of spring and the typical Japanese expression of *mono no aware* dominates the tone. He is seeing the spring gradually unfold before his eyes and he is delighted at the sight of the Sun smiling benevolently overhead. But his happiness is mellowed by sadness when he sees the cherry being blown away by the wind. This is *mono no aware*.

This is the feeling of pathos for this impermanence and transience of this beauty. Subconsciously, perhaps the poet is also lamenting his own state where he knows that his life, comfort and post will not last forever and will be blown away just by a single gush of wind like the cherry-blossoms.

34

A Great Age

Fujiwara no Okikaze

Tare o ka mo
Shiru hito ni sen
Takasago no

Matsu mo mukashi no
Tomo nara naku ni

Who is still alive,
To be called by me a friend?
Grown so old, that now I find--
The pines of Tagasako young.

Tagasako lies in the Harima Bay within the current Hyogo Prefecture and is noted for its ancient Pine forests. It also finds mention in Poem numbered 71 in this anthology. As for the poet, not much is known though he is one of the Poetry Immortals of Japan.

This poem is beautiful in the way that it laments his great age, but more so, it laments his loneliness. This loneliness may actually be the main theme of the poem and the old age that he speaks about may be completely imaginary but since we do not yet know when the Okikaze was born or when he died, we cannot comment on this interpretation. So, for the moment, we accept its meaning from what is apparent from the poem.

35

The Smell of Plum Blossoms

Ki no Tsurayuki

Hito wa isa
Kokoro mo shirazu
Furusato wa

Hana zo mukashi no
Ka ni nioi keru

The plum-blossoms are same,
As they smelled in childhood days,
Though the hearts of men I knew
Have traveled different ways.

Among the common men in this anthology, Ki no Tsurayuki deserves special mention as the compiler Japan's first Imperial anthology the *Kokin Wakashu*. This poem is also special in the sense that it speaks of the advent of spring. In Japanese literature, beginning of Spring signifies new beginning and it is the time when the poet finds himself revisiting old memories. It is then, that the poet seems to realize that before he even noticed, the "men he knew" have traveled different ways that is to say that he no longer finds them the way they were before. A feeling of desolation and loneliness sets in just when he remembers that the plum blossoms (in full bloom in early spring) are the same and that they still provide him company on his sojourn through life.

So here, the smell of the plum blossoms have a two-fold importance. Firstly, it specifies the time of the year when the poet is writing the poem and secondly, it is used as an emotional element of Spring i.e. it is used to symbolize an awakening from desolation when the poet realizes that he is not alone amidst this entire panorama of seasons.

36

The Wandering Moon

Kiyohara no Fukayabu

Natsu no yo wa,
Made yoi nagara,
Akenuru wo,

Kumo no izuku ni,
Tsuki yadoruran.

The summer night is here,
The evening still is passing,
The dawn will now break soon.
Now what cloudy shelter does
Host the wandering moon?

Fuakayabu is the progenitor of a most gifted line of litterateurs. He was the grandfather of Motosuke and the great grandfather of Sei Shonagon the author of the 'Pillow Book'. In this poem he uses his imagination to draw up a beautiful scene of the moon lodging among the clouds. The first two lines deserve special notice. The poet says, the summer night is here, but then again, the evening is still passing. He feels that it is too early for the night to set in.

Then suddenly he realizes that the dawn will break soon (summer nights being usually short). Then he gazes at the moon and observes that its about to set. He is yet not ready to accept this and imagines that the moon will be resting at some place among the clouds that adorn the western sky. This is a light-hearted poem describing the moon hiding behind the summer clouds. A reason why this was not included in the Imperial anthologies of his time which led to his downfall as a poet.

Just as all Tanka poems. this too may have another meaning at a personal level. Some scholars explain that this may also be a poem lamenting the quick passage of the poet's life. Unable to accept this fact, he uses the moon hiding behind the clouds as an allegory trying to comfort himself.

The Wandering Moon, Poem 36, Kiyohara no Fukayabu

37

The Careless Winds

Fun'ya no Asayasu

Shiratsuyu wo,
Kaze no fukishiku
Aki no no wa,

Tsuranuki tomenu,
Tama zo chiri keru.

Thousand unstrung gems,
Have scattered in the field,
As the autumn evening wind,
Blows carelessly through the yield.

The inclusion of this poem in this selective anthology is strange as scholars like Professor Mostow points out. Compared to many others, this is a relatively simple poem with very typical analogies. The dew-drops are compared to unstrung gems blown in with the autumn wind and getting scattered throughout the fields. This poem is however, comparable to Poem numbered 96 in the Ogura Hyakunin Isshu where the poet feels that his garden is turning white because of the great age that he has lived and not because the white cherry blossoms are scattering all about. Again, it may be compared to poem numbered 89 by Shokushi Naishinnō where she compares her own life to a jeweled-string. So, taking these two relations a new meaning can be brought into light regarding this poem but since there is no evidence of general usage of these analogies, they may be taken to be specific to that poem and poet.

But the current poem appears in several other anthologies in spite of being very simple and typical. Some scholars doubt a behind-the-scene influence of family and status at work.

38

The Broken Vow

Lady Ukon

Wasuraruru,
Mi wo ba omowazu
Chikaite shi

Hito no inochi no,
Oshiku mo aru kana.

I know he has forsaken me,
But he pledged before the Gods,
And for that I cannot think of
The pity--that is his life.

The title of this tanka attributes it to a certain Lady Ukon. She takes this sobriquet after her father's post which was *ukon-e no shoshoi*. Her original name yet remains unknown just as the most celebrated authoress of the word Lady Murasaki. She is said to have a great number of romantic liaisons like her father and this poem in fact proves it. It is believed that this poem she wrote to deliberately force her lover to remember his vow that he made before the gods, perhaps of never forsaking her, which he has now broken. That way this poem is in a way cruel and opens up a sadistic side to her nature though she is reported to be a kind, busy and a dedicated woman.

Another theory says that this poem was probably written as a personal note to remind herself of the way she was betrayed, perhaps as a remembrance note telling her not to fall for fake vows again In this second meaning, it sounds much less harsh but certainly more tragic than the first where the outbreak of the pain clearly finds form rather than being silently dug beneath her being.

39

My Love Remains the Same

Minamoto no Hitoshi

Asajiu no,
Ono no shinohara,
Shinoburedo,

Amaride nado ka,
Hito no koishiki.

Like growing bamboo trees,
Among those tangled reeds,
Unbearable, my hidden love
Remains for her the same.

Apparently this poem was sent to a woman in the usual tradition, written on a fan or a piece of silk. Though Hitoshi was little known in the world of poetry, Teika was not wrong to select this poem for the Ogura Hyakunin Isshu. This poem shows some impressive characteristics as a love poem. Firstly, it has a beautiful rhyming word usage. The first and third lines and again the second and fourth lines rhyme and then the fifth line breaks this alternate rhyming pattern and proclaims the end of the poem--a powerful instrument of poetry to awaken the reader back to life from the slumber of the poem.

Secondly, the poet uses a clever analogy to describe how he tries to hide his love. He compares his love's revelation to the bamboo trees that peek through the tangled reeds that grow in marshy lands. That is the poets expression of how he has to hide his love for her. Then he wants to clarify that his love remains to the same and thus he says it directly in the last line.

40

The Secret Love Appears

Taira no Kanemori

Shinoburedo,
Iro ni ideni keri
Waga koi wa,

Mono ya omou to,
Hito no tou made.

Inspite of hiding, still,
In my face, my Love appears,
And now he asks me casually,
If something is bothering me.

This poem has an interesting history on how it found its way to this anthology. It was probably written at a poetry contest held in 960 CE. Kanemori was competing against the poet of the 41st poem Mibu no Tadami. The judge(Fujiwara no Saneyori) failed to decide who the winner was, so upon consulting a greater poetry expert (Minamoto no Taka'akira), who also failed to come to reach consensus, they brought the poems before the Emperor Murakami. The emperor after reading through only the first poems (number 40) declared Kanemori the victor. This is how this poem came into the limelight (by treachery) and rose high from among the great multitude of poems written in the Heian Period of which only a hundred found its way to this anthology.

This poem is outstanding because of its simplicity and colloquial word usage for poetry that was quite rare in the Heian period.

In this poem, the author pretends to be a woman, a typical characteristic of Heian tanka poems especially if they were written for poetry competitions. Probably it were these specialities that won it an upper hand and caught the eye of the emperor.

41

The Rumor of My Love

Mibu no Tadami

Koisu cho
Waga na wa madaki
Tachi ni keri

Hito shirezu koso
Omoi someshi ka

The rumour of my love,
Though it all was true,
Had spread across the land,
But other men should not have known
That I have begun to love.

According to traditional legend, Mibu no Tadami died from the shock after losing in the poetry contest against the poet of the preceding poem. However, the existence of many other poems attributed to his name prove otherwise. Though he lost against Kanemori, this poem was greatly praised for a long time and won equal appreciation as Kanemori's.

This poem is fairly simple, though technical complexities lurk beneath the apparent obviousness. In the days of the Heian period, love and polygamy though were accepted practices, were looked down upon when it became public. An embarrassing rumour spreading through the Imperial Palace could destroy the career of a statesman. That angle is beautifully upheld in this poem where the poet laments that the news of his love should not have spread such that it has.

For the technical part referred to previously, the meaning of the poem may subtle change if we take the alternate readings and interpretations based on them. If one takes note they will see that the word *"omoi"* in the last line may both refer to the word *"shirezu"* as well as *"someshi"*. *Omoi* means "to know" or "to feel" but *omoi* with *shirezu* means something like "I though no one knew" but *omoi* with *someshi* means "I have begun to love" (so ignoring the grammar factor I have kept the line as it is in my rendering.) Then again, the entire 5th line can been taken to mean "I thought I had just begun to love her." (Reference 8) But it also should come as no surprise if the original poem had contained *"omoi someshi ga"* instead of *"ka"*, because many characters were pronounced differently later on then the line could be interpreted as "Oh? How I wish to start loving with no one knowing it". But what actually came to the mind of Tadami has long died with him and today appears as a mystic word-play to us.

42

The Pledge of Tears

Kiyohara no Motosuke

Chigiriki na
Katami ni sode o
Shibori tsutsu

Sue no matsuyama,
Nami kosaji to wa.

The tears on our sleeves,
Are proof that our love.
Will last until, Mount Sue's pines,
Are washed by ocean waves.

This poem, Motosuke claims to have written to convey the feelings of a friend rather than himself. Here, the readers witness another feature of tanka poetry: to imagine oneself in another's situation and compose the poem to convey his or her feelings. The poem numbered 21 also displays this feature where a Buddhist monk pretends to be an ardent lover.

Sue-no-matsu is a real place in the current Miyagi Prefecture, some believe it to be the same mountain that is called *sue-no-matsuyama* here (yama=mountain). It should be noted that the word *matsu* means "pine" (as well as 'to wait' when used as a verb) so basically Motosuke uses it to give a double meaning to the phrase. The idea that he wants to convey is to reassure his friend's lover (who is perhaps treating him with coldness) that his love for her will always remain no matter what happens. It seems that the poet is well assured that the high pine trees adorning Sue-no-matsuyama will never be washed away by the ocean waves. And thus his love for her will never wander.

In this poem, the poet hints at the fickleness of passion and how soon and easily it may die out like a flame in the stormy winds. Interestingly the usage of the Pines is comparable to that in the 16th poem.

43

The Feelings of the Past

Fujiwara no Atsutada

Ai mite no,
Nochi no kokoro ni,
Kurabureba,

Mukashi wa mono wo,
Omowazari keri.

Since I met my love,
And have known that I am loved,
The feelings of the past
Are meaningless to me.

These poems may or may not convey the exact feelings of the poet himself to whom the poem is attributed to. As already discussed, tanka poems most often had this peculiar characteristic of portraying another's feelings (even imaginary ones) instead of the poet's own. Nevertheless, the readers, are able to connect themselves to these feelings and imagery, even in this modern age when everything from the mantle of sociological stratification and segregation of aristocracy to the status of men and women in the society has undergone a massive change all around the world. That is what makes these poems an inseparable part of world literature whose legacy lives on all through the ages unchanged by changes all around them.

This poem, is in a way comparable to poem numbered 30 which laments the separation of the lovers and upholds the poet's strong desire for his partner. Here, though the general sense conveyed is that of a meeting that has changed the poet and reshaped his feelings, the actual point of time which the poem speaks of is the time after that (probably first) meeting has taken place. So, in reality the poet is not referring to the meeting or its recollection; but to the feelings that have nested in him after that momentary comforting glance (unmarried men and women meeting, in the days of the Heian period was of very rare occurrence and even if they did, it was often a very short affair) So, poetry was the only and accepted way in which they could converse with each other and also arrange for their meetings. And thus it also became the most common way to reflect upon such a meeting and send his or her thoughts and feelings to his or her partner.

The poems that came to be written after these momentary meetings, came to be known as "reflection tanka" that delves into the heart of a lover and expresses his deepest feelings for his or her partner. This is such a "reflection tanka" though I prefer to call it a "recollection tanka."

These reflect upon the feelings that the poet had after he (usually not she, because it was generally the man who was expected to write his thoughts) came back from the the brief meeting and often express longing desire to meet again, a chance for which, often never came. It is in this manner, that this poem shares a commonality with those of Mibu no Tadamine (30) and Fujiwara no Yoshitaka (50) and also forms an separate heading under which they can be classified.

44

I am Content

Fujiwara no Asatada

Au koto no,
Taete shi nakuwa,
Nakanaka ni,

Hito wo mo mi wo mo
Urami zaramashi.

I will not complain,
If we never meet again.
For I know that she and I,
Would never feel forsaken.

Interpretations of this poem are diverse. According to scholars of Japanese literature, only the real word-meaning of this poem should be taken note of whereas, the compiler probably saw more than just the apparent in this poem and so, decided to incorporate it into his selective anthology.

The compiler, Fujiwara no Teika believed: this was composed by Asatada after being rejected by his lover--a woman who had behaved truly coldly with him even on their first meeting. This meeting is something that the poet now detests and wishes it to drown in oblivion. So, the poet says, that neither she nor he would ever feel forsaken or even sad if they never met again in their life. He feels content to have faced that icy coldness of her once and does not wish to experience it twice.

But modern scholars believe otherwise. Unable to rely completely on Teika's imagination and general usage. They believe that the detestation that Asatada hints at his trials to meet his lover which has brought immense perturbations to his life and he wants to end them. So, he says that even if they never met, even if his attempts never bear fruit, he will not regret it and would consider it a respite from this pitiable situation.

45

The Tale's End

Fujiwara no Koremasa

Aware to mo,
Iu beki hito wa,
Omooede,

Mi no itazura ni
Narinu beki kana.

There is none to shed a tear,
And pity my lost love.
And so this story's fitting end
Must be my own non-being.

This is a desperate poem. But the desperation is not only for what normally meets the eye. Koremasa was a poet and regent to the emperor from 970 CE and was frequently involved in poetry competition judging and anthology compilation works. So, it was very normal for him to feel pressurized when competing at a poetry competition. This way, this poem has a two-fold meaning that are applicable simultaneously.

This poem was probably written to get the attention of a girl whom Koremasa loved. Writing a poem and dedicating it to a girl in an open poetry-competition was a great way to accomplish such deeds and this is precisely what the poet does. This poem has a certain sense of desperation in it and a feeling of inability to accept defeat. This defeat is both in love against the lady as well as in the poetry competition. Thus he turns to sentimental phrases to convey his desperation here.

The sense conveyed in this poem is simple. It is an expression of desperation and plight but the phrases used are carefully dressed in psychological playfulness to cause a stir in the soul of the lady as well as the judges; and this way Koremasa can truly be called a master of *waka* poetry.

46

The Disastrous Ocean of Love

Sone no Yoshitada

Yura no to o
Wataru funabito
Kaji o tae

Yukue mo shiranu
Koi no michi kana

Like a sailor in Yura's strait
Sailing with his oar-cord torn.
From this ocean of my Love,
I cannot find the shore.

Not much is known of the poet or this poem. Sone no Yoshitada, probably lived in the eleventh century and was prolific poet but his writings do not feature frequently in other anthologies. His style was perhaps considered too unconventional and thus unacceptable until Teika included thus in his selection of poems for the Hyakunin Isshu.

First of all, scholars are not yet unanimous on the location of the place *"Yura"* or *"Yura's strait"*. Two places with the same name are present in both *Kii* and *Tango* provinces.

Yoshitada being the Secretary of the Tango latter, scholars opine that it is the Yura of Tango Province that is referred to here. The rest of the poem is quite simple and uses basic imagery of being lost in the ocean of love -- a very common metaphor used in literature expressing profundity.

A little technical difficulty faced by translators and commentators working on this poem is that there exists an alternative and disputed reading of third line of this poem. It may be read as both *"kaji wo tae"*(to lose an oar) as well as, *"kaji-o tae"* (the oar-cord snaps) which gives it two sets of meanings accordingly. Most modern scholars and I myself prescribe to the latter reading and have translated the poem thus. But taking the alternate reading, the new interpretation can also be subscribed to and in that case the poem takes on a different note.

47

The Autumn Guest

Priest Egyo

Yaemugura,
Shigereru yado no,
Sabishiki ni

Hito koso miene,
Aki wa ki ni keri.

The loneliness of the cottage,
Adorned with thick vines,
Welcomes the sad autumn,
Without a man -- a host.

Priest Egyo lived and worked in the latter part of the tenth century and was hailed as the "Dhamma-master Egyo". He was a Buddhist priest and has naturally imbibed certain Buddhist philosophical sermons in this poem which was probably written as an entry to a poetry-contest. The subject on which poems had to be composed in that competition was probably "Autumn in a Lonely House" or something similar. The imagery, as well as the language usage does not demand much explanation but the underlying meaning demands it.

Before we come to that, we must take note of the fact that Egyo was well associated with contemporary poets and that they met frequently at the Kawara Mansion. Scholars are of the opinion that the house spoken about in this poem is the same Kawara Mansion.

This poem has a subtle didactic aspect to it. Though it simply paints an imagery of autumn in an empty house, it probably in reality has a Buddhist sermon intertwined with it. In spite of the fact that no one is there to play the host there, the autumn has arrived this probably wants to convey a secret message enveloped in this imagery: he says, that sadness and loneliness will haunt us and come unheralded when the time comes even if we do not welcome them or approve of them. This teaching is tactfully enshrouded by this imagery and Egyo's imagination. And this in fact is a typical aspect of Japanese poetry where there should be a double meaning and preferably a philosophical teaching entwined with picturesque description for it to qualify as a great poem; as this poem beautifully depicts.

48

The Lashing Waves

Minamoto no Shigeyuki

Kaze wo itami,
Iwa utsu nami no,
Onore nomi

Kudakete mono wo,
Omou koro kana.

The wind lashes itself,
Upon a jutting rock,
So am I, crushed on the shore
By my thoughts for her.

This poem is not so simple as it appears when the reader gets down to the intricate parts of the analogy used here. But before that, we must first take a look at the poet's background. Shigeyuki was a popular man and a prodigious poet who died sometime in the early eleventh century. He had good contacts with contemporary poets including Kanemori and Sanekata to name a few and they influenced him to a great extent. In fact this poem, to a slight extent follows from Sanekata's style (poem 51) in comparing his state of love to natural phenomenon.

The imagery is two-fold here. First the analogy (in this case, neither a metaphor nor a simile) which speaks of the waves lashing against the boulders on the coast driven by the wind. Then the second part is the poets own feelings which he relates to the waves. But the interesting part is that he doesn't speak directly of this similarity or this relation between the two. He says that he is feeling lashed and thrown onto the shore, being crushed on a boulder by his thoughts "for Her" but not even for once does he refer to the coldness of his lover.

This poem was probably composed in response to that coldness of his beloved that made him compare it to the icy cold waves of the ocean. And here the boulders in fact stand for that coldness on the part of his lover and the turbulent waves are nothing but his passion and desire for her. Which are driving him, and lashing him, crushing him under their weight on those boulders which are her lover's aloofness. So there is also a feeling of defeat or broken-hearted disillusionment associated with it; which is entwined with the feeling of rising and trying again only to meet a similar fate.

49

The Burning of My Love

Onakatomi no Yoshinobu

Mikakimori
Eji no taku hi no
Yoru wa moe

Hiru wa kie tsutsu
Mono o koso omoe

Like the burning fire at night
Of the guards at palace gates,
Turn ashes in the day
So is the love for you in me.

Comparatively a simpler poem after a series of misleading ones. Here, not only the imagery but also the language is very simple compared to the ones preceding this. The poet's love for, again, his cold lover burns like the flames at the palace gates; and just like they turn ashes in the day, his passion also subsides beneath the load of all other cares that he has to attend to throughout the day. But with the rising moon, it again takes possession of the poet--the cycle continues.

It is interesting to note, that it is because of that coldness of the woman, that her lover, writing this poem compares his love for her to the burning fire--to balance the two images. This balance (*"catharsis"*), though very important in English and European poetry, deriving their influences from Aristotle is however, not a necessary element in Japanese poetry; Haiku(s) rarely (if not never) contain it (Haiku-s have a different them underlying theme--there has to be a sharp change of imagery involved), Tanka-s have it sometimes (like the current one) but mostly they don't. So, we must assume and accept these little differences that will continue to surface in English and Japanese literature and must interpret each other in the way its own language and culture demands and not through the tinted glass of another culture or language.

50

A Broken Love

Fujiwara no Yoshitaka

Kimi ga tame,
Oshi karazarashi,
Inochi sae

Nagaku mo gana to
Omoi keru ka na

Once, for your sake, my life,
To me, it was not so dear.
But now I pray that it might have
Many more griefs to bear.

This is called a "morning after" poem by common
readers of the Ogura Hyakunin Isshu. But this may be
a more decent and modest poem than it appears as well.
"Morning after"-poems are, as discussed previously, poems
written to be sent to a lover's quarters after spending the
entire night with her. They are usually warm and speak
something about the enchanting night they had together.
But this poem is different. Usually they portray a coldness
that comes when the warmth is taken away, with the light of

the day, they have to separate; and so they share a common feeling of "parted company". The original generalized term for this genre of *waka* is *kinuginu no uta*. But this is not on equal platform with the others.

The main reason for that, is, this poem does not depict that intense longing that is a common feature of "morning after" poems. In fact it is quite the reverse and speaks of a desire to break away from that bond of love. It says that whilst he was entangled in his lover's arms, he thought that even his life was worth giving up for it. But now he has a different feeling. As soon as he met her, he understood that he couldn't leave her; yet he has to (Yoshitaka died at the age of twenty of small-pox) and thus he wants to elevate his life to a great level by saying that he wants to give away his life for her sake. This is a poem depicting deep-love and not detestation. But the colour of this love, is not deep red (like poem 17) but pure, serene and silent white. In fact, the Hyakunin Isshu is all about the different shades of Love and its different manifestations.

An Interlude: Looking Back

In this anthology, we have now already traveled half the way. But on the wings of Time, we have, in reality flown across four centuries. Starting from the fag end of the seventh, we have reached the late tenth century in this short span of fifty poems. In the remaining fifty, we will take a tour of the other three that are recorded in the Ogura Hyakunin Isshu. An interesting point is that even when we view the fiftieth poem, it is so amazing to think that Fujiwara no Teika is not even born yet. We are now probably dealing with the times of his great grandfather. These poems did not die away and lose their way into the sea of oblivion but remained there. In the imperial, personal and similar anthologies, they remained and waited for Teika to be assigned the task of gathering these hundred poems and bring them to the forefront by lifting them out of the great multitude of poem in those anthologies and placing them in this shorter and more important anthology of "a selected hundred."

So, we can safely conclude that these poems are "classics" because they have been separated, labeled and safely 'discriminated' against and claimed to belong to a different and more elevated category of poetry. All the prerequisites to safely qualify as '"*classici*"'. And that is why these poems are important in World Literature. As mentioned before, they present an insight into the Japanese social world, that general mainstream history overlooks. It provides us with a niche to delve into the of the Japanese socio-political life with first-hand accounts and at a more personal level. These are the functional advantages of the Ogura Hyakunin Isshu that it empowers us with the this ability to see the past without a coloured glass--a historians interpretation. According to me, this is the most beneficial aspect of these contextual poems in this anthology where they serve as a living account of history. In general the poems of the Hyakunin Isshu can be divided into three main categories. Namely, Contextual, Picturesque and Metaphorical. The Contextual poems are those that simply portray a context or situation which in itself forms the central and only pillar of the poem the poems numbered seven (Nakamaro's exile) and eleven (Takamura's exile) can be classified under this category. Picturesque poems are those that simply describe a beautiful scene for the sake of its beauty and does not relate it to any emotion or biographical event. The fourth poem of this anthology (Mount Fuji's Peak) is a classic example of this genre. The third category of poems are the most abundant. Almost eighty percent of the poems in the Hyakunin Isshu belong to this category. These poems mix a certain degree of imagery with a personal feeling or historical event and may at times be satyric. But the majority of the poems follow this trend due to the underlying feeling of the Japanese poets in the Heian period that poetry should also have a social and moral value and not only be for mere entertainment. This was the philosophical reason behind the didactic teachings enshrouded in that picturesque poem written by Priest Egyo.

Anyhow, whilst on our journey through these fifty poems, we have encountered poems by three emperors, one empress and about four female poets, a great multitude of state officials, three priests and another great number of

Fujiwara(s). It is interesting as well as important to note the increasing frequency of Fujiwaras in the latter half of the anthology. There are altogether nine Fujiwara poets in the first fifty poems and in the latter half the number is twelve. This hints at two important facts. One, the Fujiwara(s) were becoming more and more powerful and started to occupy greater posts in the Imperial court in the days from the tenth to the thirteenth century when they had a sudden downfall after the Genpei War; and secondly, the compiler Fujiwara no Teika also belonging to the same clan records more and more poems written by his close clan members than distant ancestors and members of other families. So altogether there are twenty-one poems by the members of the Fujiwara clan (quite a substantial number). This number twenty-one reminds us of another important class of poets who share the same number of poems in the anthology as the Fujiwara(s).

The female poets. Here is an interesting point to note, and an interesting inference to draw from the poems written by the female members of the anthology. Among the total twenty-one, only five surface in the first fifty poems. That means that only about 23% of the first 50% of the anthology is composed by women. But the number shoots up, to a startling 16 in the latter part of the anthology which brings the percentage to 32% of the latter 50%. So if we take the basic presumption that the poems in the Hyakunin Isshu were arranged roughly chronologically, then we should say that it is from the days from the late tenth century that more and more women became educated and entered the literary community. It was after all the eleventh century that produced great literary women like Murasaki Shikibu and Sei Shonagon who have left almost a permanent mark on World Literature; and so, this proposition is not totally unjustified.

We must take this opportunity to retrospect our journey through these four centuries or fifty poems and examine what we have come across and witnessed through these fifty poems. The ages that we have flown across were mainly peaceful and thus flourishing of poetry and the creative arts is a natural event in these times. But the existence of this great multitude of poems from this age can also be accredited to the influence of China and ancient Chinese philosophy and customs of the Japanese court-life during this period. The profound ties that Japan forged with China transgressed the boundaries of need and the requirements of trade and commerce but also reached out and affected the cultural and intellectual realms of Japanese life. The effect of the "Six Dynasties Style" and the essence of "Elegant Confusion" is clearly visible in poems like number 29 by Oshikochi no Mitsune (The White Chrysanthemum) and number 31 by Sakanoue no Korenori (Drifting Snow). This contact gradually however, turned hostile and ultimately ceased. The early years of this hostility fall within the purview and coverage of this anthology; and if the reader is careful might, he might spot the indigenous Japanese style in the making and early years of development. The inquisitive reader might have noticed the general change of tone and image-formation techniques that these poems portray. Emperor Tenchi's poem was entirely metamorphic and philosophical but not free from the ballad-like style of eulogizing the reigns of kings; but the poems of the latter poets beginning with Sarumaru's Autumn Stag, are more personal and more imbibed with feelings than the first few. At the height of this genre we will reach the 49th poem where the feeling of burning passion completely usurps the centre stage and even the imagery of the burning fire and the ashes are in a way directly related to that passion--the change is imminent.

Another interesting aspect to look at is Teika's compilation of the poems. He does not allow two similar sort of poems, belonging to the same genre to be placed side-by-side. A good example of that would be the 29th and the 31st poems where both have the essence of "Elegant Confusion". They are carefully separated by the 30th, a poem resembling the "morning after" or *kinuginu no uta* style. The weight of the Metaphorical poems, the first and second, is beautifully balanced by two plainly picturesque poems--the third and fourth. So, there is a masterful balance in the poetry styles and metaphors in the anthology than most others which categorize poems mainly by context and theme. So, here we must conclude that Teika was not only a master and a nobleman with high birth but also a great poet (as it shall be seen) and a great critic of poetry as well.

51

The Burning Fire-Plant

Fujiwara no Sanekata

Kaku to dani,
Eyawa ibuki no,
Sashimogusa,

Sashimo shiraji na,
Moyuru omoi wo.

Ibuki's fire-plant,
Burns amidst my heart,
Will she ever know
How fierce my longing is?

After the interlude, we return to the poems. This is
a direct or contextual poem with a slight tinge of
imagery in it. Here the essence is quite straightforward
and nothing very novel but the imagery is truly captivating
within the limits of minimalism. Ibuki probably refers to a
famous mountain in Japan--Mount Ibuki which houses a
wide variety of flora and fauna. The point of interest here,
is the "fire plant" or *"sashimogusa"*. Sashimogusa is a shrub-
like plant belonging to the Mugwort family. These plants

have a natural appearance of burning shrubs and were used in moxibution which involved burning of the plant to produce *"moxa"* used in the medical treatment. The poet uses these two characteristics of the plant to compare his burning feeling to the image of the burning plant.

Mention must be made of a special characteristic of this poem that this poem is not intended to be silently kept aside to remind the poet of his love, as is apparent from the tone of it; but was used to propose his love to her. It also acted as a poem introducing Sanekata to his lover, who probably was totally oblivious of his existence.

An interesting point to note on the language is that, there is a word-play in usage of the term "sashimo" which may also be read as *"sa shimo"* meaning "that much". Along with the words *"mogusa"* and *"omoi"* act as a tool to emphasize the passionate love.

52

The Night and Day

Fujiwara no Michinobu

Akenureba,
Kururu mono to wa,
Shiri nagara,

Nao urameshiki,
Asaborake kana.

I know that Night will chase,
The growing light of Dawn.
Yet how hateful is its light
And the day that's to be born.

Here we have another "morning after" poem or *kinu-ginu no uta*. The imagery is however similar to that of seasonal poems. In fact as per Japanese customs of poetry composition, this is a Seasonal poem or *"kisetsu no uta"* which has been condensed into the changes within a day-- the changes from Day to Night and back to Day. In fact, the most important feature and essence of seasons in Japanese literature is the transience and the changes of the seasons. They do not view them as static and unchanging but as a dynamic and living aspect of nature constantly in evolution. But here the seasonal variation has been condensed to that of a single day.

This poem portrays the situation where the the author dreads the coming of the daylight when he will be forced to return from his lover's chambers to his lonely quarter. Here again, we have the word *"Asaborake"*, already discussed in detail in poem 31, the reference is to the dawn of the winter which might be entirely metaphorical to the coldness of the separation. But one reason to take the word literally is, only on a late autumn or winter dawn would be the parting more painful because in that case, the poet would have greater time with his lover and the outside world would appear too cold for his elated heart.

But in the end, Michinobu knows that another night will follow this cold day and that this parting is not eternal separation. This effect of the day chasing the night is the same as the effect of the cycle of seasons where the poet is always reminded that the Winter is followed by the Spring.

53

A Night of Emptiness

The Mother of Michitsuna

Nageki tsutsu,
Kitori nuru yoru no,
Akuru ma wa,

Ikani hisahiki
Mono to ka wa shiru.

Alone have I lain,
Counting hours of darkness,
Until the break of daylight.
Can you at all imagine--
The emptiness of that night?

This poem is truly sad. It is an example of an entirely contextual poem. Incidentally, it carried no name only the identity of the poet as the "mother of Michitsuna" who is also the author of the *"Gossamer Years"*. This poem is sad because it silently complains of her husband's unfaithfulness. The records from the *"Kagero Nikki"*--her diary claims that her husband used to sneak out of the house at night and spent it with a lover. This aggrieved his wife a lot. But keeping to the laws of her times she could not do anything but to plead her case to her husband. It is believed that, in that attempt she wrote this poem to remind him of her plight. The beauty of the versification and interesting story behind it, probably won Teika's attention and he included it in his anthology.

Here the attribution is deserves mention. This poem is neither anonymous nor does it have a poet's name attached to it. This is strange when it comes to Japanese poetry. Here, this intentional exclusion of the name of the poet might be to emphasize her role as the mother and subsequently the role of her husband as the father of Michitsuna who perhaps acts as the only bond between them. So, even in the naming, the poet has left a silent mark of her complaint.

54

My Life Must End

Gido Sanshi no Haha

Wasureji no
Yukusue made wa
Katakereba

Kyo o kagiri no
Inochi to mo gana

My live now here must end,
If remembering me
In the distant future, for him
Too difficult, it be.

The poem is attributed to *"Gido Sanshi no Haha"* or the "Mother of the Supernumerary Grand Minister" (referring to Fujiwara no Korechika). She, in reality was a woman called Takado (also mentioned as 'Kishi') and was the mother of Empress Teishi and the influential Fujiwara no Kerechika.

Talented poet, Takado came into the limelight winning a number of poetry competitions and won the favor of many a court-noble. Finally she consented to marry Fujiwara no Michitaka--an ambitious and rising noble shortly after which she wrote this poem.

This poem can be misleading on first reading. It has no sad or emotionally forlorn perspective to it. It was composed out of the joy of marriage and prays for a happy married life. The aspect of the life ending used here is not in the literal sense but entirely the implied meaning should be taken. Here, the poet desires to end her life, if her husband should be enchanted by another woman in future years. Its a satirical way of praying for a happy married life.

Sadly, her life did not turn out to be as she desired. Michitaka passed away leaving her a widow and she is said to have taken to Buddhism and became a nun.

55

The Silent River

Fujiwara no Kinto

Taki no ota wa,
Taete hisashiku,
Narinuredo,

Na koso nagarete,
Nao kikoe kere.

The waterfall has died.
No longer does it flow.
Its name has traveled far and wide,
Though silent, long ago,
Its sound is said to blow.

F ujiwara no Kinto is one of the poets whom Teika could not afford to miss out. He was the selector of the "Thirty-Six Immortals of Poetry" and the compiler of several waka anthologies which symbolize Japanese poetry to this date. Thus, he was the absolute authority in poetry at his time. A prolific poet himself, he got his poems included in several of the anthologies and the Ogura Hyakunin Isshu is just one of them.

This poem is said to have been written close to Mount Ogura. It was written after Kinto visited a Buddhist temple named *Daikakuji* (near Ogurayama) and has deep-lain Buddhist philosophy in it. During late Heian period, Buddhism had made quite an astonishing progress into Japan and this poem bears proof of this influence.

The waterfall, which symbolized life with all its ups and downs is shown to be dead and silent. It actually refers to physical death here. But what Kinto desires to say is that the actions and tales of Man's deeds go far and wide and thus he may live on even after his life. This a more Hindu aspect but considering the links that Buddhism shared with Hinduism, its no surprise to find its essence in medieval Japan.

The imagery of the waterfall being silent is the death of man and again brings the Buddhist concept of impermanence and transience into existence that forms the basis of the Japanese world-view so from this time onward, we can see the clear distinct Japanese style and philosophy and a divorce from Confucian ethics and beliefs.

56

The Last Words

Lady Izumi

Arazaran,
Kono yo no hoka no,
Omoide ni,

Ima hitotabi no,
Au koto mo gana.

When soon now I will be
Beyond this mortal world,
I know I will forget.
But let me now know only this--
Our last and final meeting.

Lady Izumi is one of the most prolific poets of the
Hyakunin Isshu and surely one of the most noteworthy
female poets perhaps after Lady Murasaki and Sei
Shonagon. Given the great variation of good and bad times
she had through her life, it would not be a misjudgment
to claim that she had leaned a lot through her life and her
poetry reflects those lessons. She won the favor of many a

court-noble and the detestation of several noble women in the Heian court including Lady Murasaki herself.

This poem is biographical and relates to her relationship outside marriage. Unhappy with her marriage with Tachibana no Michisada, she left him and met Prince Tametaka, the son of Emperor Reizei, in secret. This enraged Michisade and he left her, after which she married Tametaka who died early due to a plague. A widow, Lady Izumi attracted the attention of Tametaka's brother Atsumichi. The relationship was discovered and Atsumichi's wife left him in disgust. Eventually, Lady Izumi moved in with Atsumichi but he died at the age of 27. Devastated, Lady Izumi spent her days among the inner circle of Empress Shoshi where she came in contact with other prodigious poets and authors including Lady Murasaki(poem 57) and Akazome Emon (poem 59) though as is revealed in Lady Murasaki's diary, she was not a very great poet as per Murasaki's standards.

So, the point in relating her life's ups-and-downs is that Lady Izumi was one woman who faced several pains throughout her life and that it may described to be, if I be allowed to use the word, stratified. This poem included in the Hyakunin Isshu by Teika is placed very close by to the one praying for a happy married life by Kinto (poem 54) and this one is written by a woman who never quite enjoyed a long and happy married life. So, perhaps in Teika's compiling, there is a sense of irony as well as a didactic preaching.

This poem intends to teach the reader that all good things must come to an end because it was written in her final days and desires earnestly to see 'someone' for the last and final time. However, scholars are yet not sure who this person might be, it may be a friend, but the language suggests that it is likely a lover or even might be her previous husbands. This teaching however, is entirely a reader-response and may not be taken as a literal truth. But to understand the poem properly, I think an understanding of the various rises and falls of Izumi's life needs the overall insight as I have tried to provide.

57

In the Shadow of the Moon

Murasaki Shikibu

Mehuri aite,
Mishi ya sore tomo,
Wakanu ma ni,

Kumo-gakure ni shi,
Yowa no tsukikage.

I surely do not know, back then
If truly He had crossed my path,
A gloomy cloud had hid the Moon
And cast a shade upon the earth.

And so we reach the most noteworthy poem in the Hyakunin Isshu composed by the most famous litterateur of Heian Japan--Murasaki Shikibu or Lady Murasaki. She is known all over the world as the first novelist, the author of the *"Genji Monogatari"* or the "Tale of Genji" but besides that, she was also a great poet and a great personality and stood out among the other Heian court ladies.

This poem is in a sense beautiful, lyrical, picturesque as well as mysterious to a certain extent. This is claimed to have been written remembering an old acquaintance from her childhood. But whether that was an old friend or some old lover, scholars are yet not sure. Legend says that she saw this mysterious person at a glance while they raced through the palace halls. But she could not see who this person because at that moment a cloud had covered the moon and cast a shade upon the Earth as the poem says. But later, contemplating the silhouette image that she had seen, Murasaki was drawn to believe that it was an old acquaintance (or perhaps a lover) who crossed her path that night.

This poem is quite interesting because it captures that fleeting essence of things, again a predominantly Japanese and to a certain extent Buddhist world-view, which we have witnessed in the process of development over the ages through the poems in this anthology. And yet again, instead of an isolated and typically pessimistic view (poem 95) about this impermanence, Murasaki happens to enjoy it to a certain extent. The tone of the poem tells us that she is perhaps cherishing the idea that he "might" be the person she wanted to see. And thus, she doesn't want to "surely know" know who it actually was lest her belief be proven wrong. So, this is a new romantic addition to the old feeling of *"mono no aware"* and this we shall see growing in the journey further down the ages into the Kamakura period.

Another interesting point to note in this poem is the use of the last word. It is a truly mysterious way in which she uses the word *"Tsukikage"*. *Tsukikage* might mean the moonlight; but it may be expanded to mean *Tsuki no Kage* which is "shadow of the Moon"-- a truly romantic and mysterious term. And this intensifies the mysterious ambiance already created through the poem manifold.

Murasaki Shikibu -- a likeness.

58

How Could I Forget?

Daini no Sanmi

Arimayama
Ina no sasawara,
Kaze fukuba,

Ide soyo hito wa,
Wasura ya wa suru.

When, from Arimayama,
Through Ina's bamboo fields,
The whistling wind blows
So it is. But,
How can I forget you?

To say that the poet of this poem was the daughter of Lady Murasaki would perhaps be enough to account for its beauty. In the translated version, the fourth line may seem to be unnecessary but as we shall later discuss, it is the most important line in the entire poem. Simple at first sight, as most of the Japanese poems, this as well has several layers of meanings that the reader needs to decode. Beginning with the biographical aspect, the poet had been in love with a Court noble Michitsuna for quite some time. But gradually Michitsuna became cold to her and she felt more and more uneasy as the relationship ensued. This poem was sent to Michitsuna as a reminder that the poet still loves him though his coldness makes her feel uneasy. The coldness is beautifully described by the mention of the winds blowing from the Mount Arima (located to the north of Kobe) which would naturally be cold.

Sanmi, uses another very curious device in this poem that is seldom found in other poems of the Hyakunin Isshu--Onomatopoeia. She uses the word *"soyo"* in the fourth line which may be translated as "So it is" and may be considered to be a linker between the analogy and the actual feeling. But this word *soyo* is also used here to imitate the whistling sound the wind makes while blowing through bamboo-grass. And this whistling sound also conveys the feeling of uneasiness that Sanmi is feeling in her relationship with Michitsuna. This novel usage makes this distinguishes this poem from the other and renders it different from the other. This, could of course be expected from such an illustrious personality such as Daini no Sanmi—the daughter of Lady Murasaki.

It should be mentioned here that Daini no Sanmi was the sobriquet used by the poet and it was actually the post that her father held at the Imperial Court. In fact, all the ladies in the anthology used sobriquets or similar origins except perhaps Lady Murasaki.

59

The Lonely Night Passes

Ekazome Emon

Yasurawade
Nenamashi mono o
Sayo fukete

Katabuku made no
Tsuki o mishi kana

I should have slept care-free
Rather than wait, in vain.
Just to see the lonely moon
Descend unto the plain.

An interesting point to note among these poems starting from the 56th, till the 61st in this series are all composed by female poets who knew each other. They were mostly employed in the circles of Empress Shoshi and were critiques of each others as well. As far as Ekazome Emon is concerned, she was both severely criticised as well as called to be the "most accomplished [poet]" by Lady Murasaki thus adding to her pride and position. She in indeed a great poet who composed poetry seriously not like the other poets who merely did it for fun.

This poem is, in a way, mysterious. Its headnote claims that she composed this for her sister who had a relationship with the Middle Regnant Michitaka. We are talking of an era when the court nobles used to live in separate quarters and it was difficult for the men and women in love to meet each other. Meetings arranged through poetry was the only way one could do it and this poem relates to such an incident. It is said, that Michitaka did not keep his promise to come and turned her down and as a result perhaps she asked her elder sister to compose a poem sarcastically remind him of his promise and tell him of her plight but that remains a mystery to this date. In that sense, this poem can well qualify as a morning-after poem or *kinuginu no uta* but nobody knows it for sure yet.

Some sources claim that this poem was not composed by Emon at all but that debate is unnecessary here. It is advisable to go in the direction where Teika hints us to.

The Lonely Night Passes, Poem 60, Ekazome Emon.

60

The Bridge of Heaven

Ko-Shikibu no Naishi

Oeyama
Ikuno no michi no,
To kereba,

Made fumi mo mizu,
Ama no hashidate.

Beyond Mount Oe's ridge,
And the far Ikuno plain,
A glimpse of Heaven's bridge,
I sorely wish to gain.

The poet Ko-shikibu no Naishi was the daughter of Lady Izumi of the 65th poem and she too was a hand-maiden of Empress Shoshi like her mother. She died young and thus there are only a handful poems attributed to her in the Imperial anthologies.

This poem was composed during a poetry competition held in the capital while the poet's mother the legendary Lady Izumi was sent to the province of Tango. One of the court nobles, the middle councilor Sadeyori teased her saying that perhaps she has sent word to Tango and asked for her mother's help but the messenger has not arrived yet. As a reply to this, Lady Ko, caught Sadayori's sleeve and composed this poem on spot.

Heaven's bridge, in this poem is *"Ama no Hashidate"* which is a natural bridge on Mizayu Bay located in modern north Kyoto prefecture and is considered one of the Three Scenes of Japan. The most interesting aspect of this poem is that it lists three famous places in the Tango prefecture in correct geographical order. Moreover, the poet enriches the content of the poem punning on the words *iku* and *fumi*. "Iku" may be used for Ikuno (the plain) but also means "to go" and so this gives a sense of desire to go to Ikuno connecting these two aspects. Again the word *"fumi"* may be interpreted to mean a letter or sentence (may be taken to mean a message) as well as "to step" therefore, again giving a sense of desire to go and visit her parents in Tango. It was actually these puns that makes this poem noteworthy. By this interesting use of the puns the poet is also developing a sense of double entendre necessary for poems composed in poetry competitions. It is said, that being ashamed of this magnificent poem, Sadeyori ran away from the contest instead of composing another poem in reply. Such was the greatness of this gifted poet who unfortunately died at a very young age.

61

The Magnificent Cherry Blossom

Lady Ise no Tayu

Inishiye no,
Nara no miyako no,
Yae-sakura,

Kyo kokonoe ni
Nioi nuru kana.

The eight-fold Cherry trees,
Of Nara -- the ancient throne,
Have bloomed and shed their fragrance
On our nine-fold palace halls.

Lady Ise no Tayu was another lady in waiting serving Empress Shoshi. This poem is picturesque but also portrays a great sense of historical-biographical aspects in it. But first we need to get the jargon of this poem clarified. The eight-fold here both refer to 'magnificence' as well as a Buddhist tenet of the path to ideal life. Legend claims that a Buddhist monk had brought an offering of cherry blossoms (or, perhaps an eight-petaled Cherry blossom) to the Empress' father Fujiwara no Michinaga. Empress

Shoshi's handmaidens were asked to compose a poem as a token of thanks to him which resulted in this composition. It is also said, that it was Lady Murasaki who was actually asked to compose this poem but she in return asked Tayu to write it for her.

In this *tanka*, an interesting point to note is the use of the character "八" which may either mean "*hachi*" or eight as well as "*yae*" meaning double. This perplexes the reader because the resultant reading may well be "double cherry" or even "eight-fold cherry". I pertain to the latter because the "eight-fold" path (Sanskrit: *Ashtangikamarga*) is also symbolic of the Buddhist theological perspective of the path to salvation and since this poem was composed to be gifted to a Buddhist priest who brought the gift of flowers, it is the only natural implied meaning to me.

Another beautiful word usage in this poem is the use of the word "*kokonoe*" in the fourth line which both mean "nine-fold" as well as the "Imperial Palace" and the poet also puns on this word by equating the two implying the metaphorical sense of the Palace being nine-fold (because of the similarity in the Kanji characters). Another interesting meaning that can be drawn from these two puns is that Tayu wants claims that the new capital Heian-kyo (Kyoto) has surpassed the ancient capital Nara in splendor and therefore the reference to the eight-fold, referring to magnificence, and the new palace as "nine-fold" or of even greater magnanimity. However, this theory lacks support and thus may just be considered an after-thought or reader-response; after all, Tankas were never meant to have one meaning.

The Magnificent Cherry Blossom,
Poem 61, Lady Ise no Tayu.

62

A Failed Excuse

Sei Shonagon

Yo wo komete,
Tori no sorane wa,
Hakaru tomo

Yo ni Osaka no,
Seki wa yurusaji.

The rooster crowed
In the midnight and had
Deceived the hearers well.
But here at the Gate of Osaka
The guards can always tell.

Sei Shonagon is yet another of the great female poets who dominated this stage. She was among the inner circles of Empress Teishi but probably was well acquainted with Lady Murasaki and her contemporaries. This poem class for a story that beings in China's Han-ku gate and ends in the poets bed-chamber.

It is said that when the Lord of Meng-Chang, advisor to the Chinese state of Qi, was taken prisoner in the neighboring state of Qin, he managed to escaped by bribery and disguising in fox-fur; however, soon his escape was discovered and Lord Zhou's troops came chasing after him. Meanwhile he reached the gates of the city at Han-ku and found them closed for it was still night-time. At this difficult hour, it was his faithful ally who imitated the crowing of a cock and made the other cocks nearby imitate it as well. In that cacophony of rooster's crowing, the guards of the gate were mislead to believe that the dawn was soon approaching and thus open the gates to the city. It was such that the Lord escape back into the safety of his home-province of Qi.

Though this poem deserves this story this is not the end of it. There is another story surrounding this poem. It is said that Sei Shonagon was often visited by the First Councilor Yukinari. Once, Yukinari left early, long before dawn by imitating the rooster's cry. The following morning he sent a poem to her saying that though against his wishes, he had to leave early fearing the approaching dawn. But most likely, the poet caught him lying. And she sent this poem as a reply mentioning that his lame excuse has been exposed.

This story is the background for the poem and the former, for the allusion of the Guards being deceived. Here, the poet intentionally makes a reference to the Osaka-Barrier or *Osaka no Seki* which may also be translated as "Gate of Meeting Hill" which is a barrier located to the east of Kyoto on the main high-way. So in this poem she eloquently states the fact that though the Chinese guards were fooled, the ever-ready sentinels at the Gate of Meeting Hill (and to the gateway t her heart) can always tell if it has been lied to.

63

I Might Tell You Myself

Fujiwara no Michimasa

Ima wa tada,
Omoi taenan,
Ta bakari wo,

Hitozute nara de,
Iu yoshi mo gana.

I regret not my wish
To break my love for you.
But all I crave for is a way
I may, tell this to you.

This poem is truly sad. It is said that Fujiwara no Michimasa, (the son of Koremasa) was in love with the High-Priestess of Ise Grand Shrine. The Grand-Shrine of Ise is dedicated to the the Sun-Goddess Amaterasu Omi-Kami and is often related with the Imperial family in many ways who claim divine descent from the Sun-goddess. It was the tradition to appoint the daughter of the reigning Emperor as the High-Priestess there and this tradition still continues in some form or the other where some member of the Imperial family is appointed the Chief Priest/Priestess at this most holy shrine.

The then High Priestess of Ise was the daughter of the retired Emperor Sanjo who was enraged at the news of this affair for the priestess was expected to remain a vestal virgin during her period of service--a practice parallel to that of the ancient priestesses of Rome; and appointed guards at the entrance to the shrine to stop Michimasa from entering it.

The unfortunate Michimasa thus decided to break his love for her. In this poem, the poet is lamenting for a way by which he might tell the Priestess himself of his decision and bid adieu to her in person and not through a letter or through some other representative agent.

64

The Breaking Dawn of Winter

Fujiwara no Sadeyori

Asaborake,
Uji no kawagiri,
Taedae ni,

Araware wataru,
Seze no ajirogi.

The mist on Uji lifts
As it clear the shallow stakes
Of fishing nets appear.
The dawn of winter breaks

Fujiwara no Sadayori was the son of the famous critique Fujiwara no Kinto and this poem included in the Hyakunin Isshu clearly belongs to the brocade of Picturesque poems in the anthology. The description is simple yet captivating--a characteristic feature of Japanese *tanka* poems describing a scenery. The only explanation required here is the meaning of the word "stakes" or *ajirogi* here which refers to the fence or weir-like structures on the water which aid in fishing by restricting the movements of the fishes. It seems that river Uji is quite often associated with fog and mist throughout Japanese literature. We have encountered the term "Uji" for Mount Uji *(Ujiyama)* in the 8th poem where Kisen refers to Uji as a mountain of gloom which may also be a mystical reference to mist; but nothing can be clearly said.

This poem, on a general level is the description of the dawn breaking over Uji river as the poet must have seen in his days. But the river Uji, along with the mist and the fishing-stakes make up a mystic imagery that is very overwhelming indeed.

Lastly, the Uji river, also called the Yodo river (75 km) rises from Lake Biwa in Shiga Prefecture and runs through the south-east of Kyoto (as Kisen mentions) and through the present Osaka Prefecture and drains into the Osaka Bay.

65

My Name Marred By Love

Lady Sagami

Uramiwabi
Hosanu sode da ni,
Aru mono wo,

Koi ni kuchinan,
Na koso oshikere.

Worse than your hate
That wets my sleeves with tears,
Or the coldness and this misery;
Is the loss of my good name.

This poem follows the trend of the 18th poem (If I Visit in Dreams) and the poem by Michitsuna's Mother (poem 53). In fact it is a combination of both. Toshiyuki Fujiwara's poem (no. 18) complains of the close-knit public scrutiny in the court of Heian Japan and the 53rd poem complains of the disloyalty of the poet's husband. Here, Lady Sagami complains of her name being polluted by an broken affair or perhaps an unfaithful husband. Her reputation is marred, she says, and in fact this is due to the disloyalty of her lover and the close-knit society of the time inside the Imperial Court. So it seems that the problem of public scrutiny did not die down between the times of Toshiyuki and Sagami. The reference to the sleeves is important here because it was a classical technique employed by Japanese *waka* poets (relation may also be drawn from 1st, 15th and 95th poems) and it portrays a sense of solitary sadness or sobbing. Here the reference is quite clear as it clearly states that the sleeves are wet with tears, but in most other poems the relation is implied. But in spite of its simplicity this poem is a masterpiece in itself; beautiful enough to draw Teika's attention to it. In fact this segment, from the 65th to the 68th poem there are a number of similar poems complaining of their status being foiled because of an unlucky love-affair.

66

My Only Friend

Abbot Gyoson

Morotomo ni
Aware to omoe
Yama-sakura

Hana yori hoka ni
Shiru hito mo nashi

On this mountain slope,
Lonely and in silence.
Stand you, Oh! Cherry tree.
No one knows me better
Than you--my only friend.

The poem is attributed to *Daisojo Gyoson* which roughly translates into Abbot or even Archbishop Gyoson. His approximate dates are 1055 to 1135 so we can clearly see that we have entered into the early 12th century. This poem is quite simple however what perplexes the readers is the headnote that says the this poem was composed when the poet saw cherry blossoms unexpectedly at Omine. Whether it was the place or the time that made the cherry unexpected is unknown. Anyhow, this poem is confusing because, Gyoson is reportedly a famous author of his time; he is even mentioned by the 14th century Buddhist monk and essayist Yoshida Kenko in his *"Essays in Idleness"* so it is not possible that no one knew of him in the world.

People say that this poem can only be completely understood by people who live in the mountains. But some also have a different explanation to this 'unexpected' reference in the headnote. They opine that though *"omoi no kakezu"* may mean 'unexpectedly' it may also be thought to mean "pleasant surprise" and then again *"omoikaku"* means to 'fall in love'. Thus it may be that Gyoson had expected to see only pine trees while climbing Mount Omine and suddenly found an *"yamazakura"* (mountain cherry that predominantly grows on the slopes of Mount Yoshino) which was a pleasant surprise to him.

However, this poem may also have a deeper meaning attached to it, given the mystical aspects of the mountain in question. Mount Omine is that the people climbing it are obliged not to speak of what they saw after coming back. They have to take take a vow to maintain this secrecy. So, this poem might mean that that the poet has seen some unsurpassable scenery and wishes to relate it to someone but unable to do so because of his vow narrates the scenery to this cherry tree. Anyhow this poem gives a sense solitary bliss and recollection of loneliness which though desolate is in itself is a very rich feeling.

67

A Ruined Reputation

Lady Suo

Haru no yo no
Yume bakari naru
Tamakura ni

Kainaku tatan
Na koso oshi kere.

If my head is lain
For a moment as short
As a spring night's dream
Upon his arm--that innocent pillow
Will be the deathbed of my name.

The stories associated with these poems included in the anthologies always seem fascinating. This poem is attributed to Lady Suo who worked as a handmaiden to some Empress of noblewomen in the Heian court. In reality this poem follows almost directly from the 65th one (Marred by Love) but this one has that background story that makes it stand apart from other similar poems that predominate this region of the anthology.

It is said, that once there was a gathering at the *Nijo-In*(Woman's Quarter in the Imperial Palace). When all the women were comfortably relaxing, Lady Suo expressed a desire to have a pillow. At that moment Fujiwara no Tadaie happening to walk by, heard her plea and stuck his hand through the curtains and asked her to take it as a pillow. Lady Suo, immediately composed this poem as a reply and sent it off to Tadaie. Here, the poet does not use the normal word for arm (*kaian*) but puns on it and uses the word "*Kainaku*" which means "pointless" whereby she means to say that putting her head on his hand will be extremely pointless which will though give her comfort, will rob her of he reputation.

So, the main difference between the Lady Sagami's and Lady Suo's poems are that though the previous one was literal, this poem is more of a joke than a real expression of plight as is the 65th poem. These poems more than anything express the variety of subjects and situations for which people in Heian Japan composed poems.

68

The Midnight Moon

Emperor Sanjo

Kokoro ni mo
Arade ukiyo ni
Nagaraeba

Koishikaru beki
Yowa no tsuki kana

Though against my wishes
I remain in this world.
But if I do, let me just know
This Moonlight and this midnight.

This anthology began with the poem by one emperor in the Nara period--a truly caring emperor, Tenchi. Even in its course it has witnessed several emperor and a few empresses but this emperor is different. By Sanjo's time, the emperor had lost his stand and became slightly more than a figurehead, a puppet in the hands of his ministers. Emperor Sanjo was in the control of his extremely powerful courtier Fujiwara no Michinaga the father of Empress Shoshi. Michinaga forced Emperor

Sanjo to abdicate in favor of his own grandson (the later Emperor Goichijo). Moreover, the failing health of the emperor forced him to abdicate a mere five years after coronation and spend the rest of his life in nearly complete isolation. Thus, his life can well be imagined to be without any great aspiration or motivation--ideal situation where such thoughts can creep in as is portrayed in this poem. In fact, the later poems in the anthology display a more casual and and laid-back period. Political diplomacy replaced the enthusiasm of the earlier ages. The emperor happily disposed off all his responsibilities formerly vested upon the throne and the Fujiwara clan took charge of administration of the land.

This poem is thought to have been composed towards the end of the emperor's life when he suffered frequently from diseases and weakness, or else, before his abdication. Here the emperor's admiration for the moon is neither sudden, not out-of-place. Perhaps there never any real real moon that the Emperor saw and marveled at. It is a traditional style of Poetry and typical imagery that the poet uses here where his sadness is related to the Moon and that too of the midnight hour.

The Moon in the Hyakunin Isshu is related to several images of many different genres. Here the Moon is equated with the sadness of the Emperor. In other poems, it is related to the coldness of parting in Morning-after poems. Other poems may find it in relation with the autumn scenery.

The moon is given different names in different situations and the phase. roughly coinciding with linguistic parallels. The most commonly used names are listed below:

Ariake : The moon during sunrise usually associated with *Asaborake*.

Shingetsu : The new moon.

Tsugomori : The last day of the lunar cycle.

Mikazuki : The crescent moon.

Mangetsu : Full moon.

Mochiduki : Full moon--an alternative old name.

Izayoizuki : Moon of the 16th day of the lunar cycle.

Tachimachizuki : Moon of the 17th day of the lunar cycle.

Fushimachizuki : Waning moon usually the half moon of this phase.

Nemachizuki : Another word for *Fushimachizuki*.

69

The Brocade of Maple Leaves

Dhamma-Master Noin

Arashi fuku
Mimoro no yama no
Momijiba wa

Tatsuta no kawa no
Nishki nari keri.

The sweeping stormy winds,
From Mount Mimoro weaves,
Adorning Tatsuta river
With a brocade of crimson leaves.

This poem is quite similar to that written by Ariwara no Narihara (poem 17) which also describes the Tatsuta river being being adorned with Maple leaves. But this poet (originally Tachibana no Nagayasu who took tonsure at the age of 26) was not a court poet or nobleman and thus does not include intricate word-play which was a typical court etiquette. This one merely described the scenery of the river being coloured red by autumn leaves blown away by the storm from the mountain peak. The word used here for storm--"*Arashi*" is also found in the 22nd poem (The Destroyer) by Fun'ya no Yasuhide. Written as a combination of the two Kanji characters for 'mountain' and 'wind' it can be ideally translated as 'Mountain-Wind' which would be the most apt translation here however I retain the usual meaning of the word which was also used in the other poem.

These description poems were an important part of Japanese society for it allowed the commoners and the nobility alike to delve into the world that they never saw for themselves. In those days, it was difficult even for the nobility to undertake a journey to the mountains which were quite expensive as well. So they could rejoice the scenery through these description composed in verse by the traveling men (as in this case, monks were ideal having no duties or obligations at a fixed place). These poems are usually very detailed and vivid enough to stir the imagination of the reader and make them 'almost see it with their own eyes.'

Mount Mimoro is located in the Nara Prefecture in the Ikaruga Village and Tatsuta river also flows thorough the Nara prefecture which was still the centre of Japanese culture even in the Heian Period. Mount Mimoro as well as the Tatsuta river are said the be seasonal dwellings of the Gods which is perhaps the reason why Noin undertook the journey as a pilgrimage.

70

The Darkening Autumn

Dhamma-Master Ryosen

Sabishisa ni,
Yado wo tachi idete
Nagamureba

Izuko mo onaji,
Aki mo yugure.

I look around myself,
When my lonely hut I leave
All around it is the same--
Dark, the autumn eve.

Monks are often found to reflect upon the nature of a scenery in a deeper and more contemplative way than other poets. It is interesting to note that while the previous section of the anthology was largely composed by noblewomen, this part has more monks and men who renounced the world, and thus had more time to enjoy the beauty of the world than the numerous noblemen found in the Hyakunin Isshu. This poem is in itself a masterpiece. Not only does it reflect upon the state of the mind but includes other images in relation to it. The lonely hut, going away, the autumn, the sunset all depict the scenery of the world declining into winter.

The poet leaving the autumn hut signifies stepping into an unknown terrain and that unknown terrain is the Winter landscape. That winter landscape is approaching and the world is darkening--metaphorically transforming into scenery of Death. So the Autumn is a threshold to that world of Death and the the sunset is also a threshold to the night--another manifestation of Dormancy which is again rooted in the mind of the poet in the form of Melancholy.

The Buddhist aspects and views also find place in this poem. The world declining into dormancy, melancholy and sadness are all aspects related to the tenets of Buddhism-- the faith of the poet and thus the admixture of Buddhist and classical Japanese elements is beautifully portrayed in this poem. The scenery of Autumn where the pathos and sadness sets in is very common in Japanese literature. And the melancholia of the autumn world is also captured in the same context. A truly genius work of poetry probably written far away from the boisterous poetry-circle of the capital.

71

The Wandering Winds

Dainagon Minamoto no Tsunenobu

Yu sureba,
Kodota no inaba,
Otozurete

Ashi no maroya ni,
Akikaze zo fuku.

Evening sets in,
Through rice leaves at my door,
The autumn wind blows.
And at my humble gate
It knocks and in it goes.

M inamoto no Tsunenobu lived in through the 11th century and had a number of poets in family who are recorded in the Hyakunin Isshu. This poem is another of the comparatively simple poems like the one by Noin (poem 69) which include no wordplay. It describes a perfect autumn scenery employing the imagery of the wind blowing through the rice leaves. The rice leaves also involve the scenery of the autumn harvest and altogether give a mesmerizing effect of and add calmness to the poem.

It is believed by scholars like Professor Mostow that this poem was composed when Tsunenobu visited his friend Minamoto no Morokata at a villa in Umezu (then located in the outskirts of the capital Kyoto). While Tsunenobu gazed at the scenery and marveled at its beauty, he composed this poem to capture it through his poetry. This might also be a poem gifted to Morokata thanking him for hosting the poets visit but such claims cannot be supported by facts yet.

However, the headnote of this poem says that it was composed on the topic: Countryside and Autumn Wind. Still, there are disputes as to the real meaning of this poem. It is an early example of a style of poetry that describes a certain landscape, known as *Jokeika* that developed around this time. There are several inconsistencies in the readings of this poem by different scholars regarding word-meanings etc. The meaning portrayed here has been deemed the most probable and thus I do not wish to weigh down the commentary by including other interpretations.

Anyhow, this poem perhaps most successfully captures the picturesque scenery of the cold wind blowing through the autumn rice field and reminds us of the first poem in the anthology by Emperor Tenchi composed about four centuries ago. I believe this not only portrays the eternal beauty of Nature but also the love that Japanese people had for Nature throughout the ages is also beautifully portrayed through this relation.

72

I Cannot Come to You

Lady Kii

Oto ni kiku
Takashi no hama no
Adanami wa

Kakeji ya sode no
Nure mo koso sure

Known all over the land,
The waves of Takashi's beach,
But if I do go near that shore,
I'll surely wet my sleeves.

This poem is attributed to *"Yushi Naishinno-ke no Kii"* or 'Kii of Princess Yushi's Circles'. For simpler reference I used just "Kii" in the title which seems to be either her name or her sobriquet. She served in the circles of Princess Yushi who was the daughter of Taira no Tsunekata. Several anthologies include Kii's poems though very little is known of her personal life.

It is said that this poem was composed in a poetry competition held by the retired Emperor Horikawa. This poem beautifully expressed the feeling of being afraid of new love and conceals this with a very clever yet beautiful metaphor. Takeshi's beach is probably located in the Osaka Bay near the modern day Takechi City located within the Osaka Metropolitan Area.

This poem was presented at the "Love-Letter Competition" held in 1102.

The metaphor of wetting her sleeves is actually the same fear that is expressed in the poems 65 and 67. The poet pretends to be afraid that her affair might be discovered and become a public issue owing to the strict scrutiny that the Heian court officials faced. The "wetting of sleeves" may refer to the drowning of her (or her lover's) reputation or perhaps the fear of being too much influenced by this love (the sleeves wetting her sleeves even if she went near.)

In a poetry competition, it was the general custom to write a poetry in reply to one by his or her opponent. An interesting fact to note is that, the poem that she was replying to is said to have been written by none other than Fujiwara no Teika's grandfather Toshitada -- and perhaps verily this was the reason why he included this poem in his anthology though it is perfectly a masterpiece by its own right. It is also interesting to note that as per legend at that time Lady Kii was almost 70 years old. It is really marvelous how she expresses the feeling of young love even at her age.

73

Behold the Cherry Blossoms

Gon-Chunagon Oe no Masafusa

Takasago no,
Onoe no sakura,
Saki ni keri

Toyama no kasumi,
Tatazu mo aranan.

I fear the mist should rise,
From the hills and hide the scene
Of the cherries blooming on mountain slopes
Far away. Below the peak.

This poem takes us deep into the early 12th century, and brings before the eyes a beautiful scenery from Japan's *Hanami* festival. Hanami is celebrated during the spring-time and involves cherry-blossom viewing. This poem dates from almost the same time as the previous one, Masafusa being a close confidant of Emperor Horikawa in retirement who held the poetry contest for Kii's poem. This also signifies that we have entered into the age of Fujiwara no Teika and the poems included hereafter will be of his associated instead of poets whom he has never known. Perhaps this is the reason why the following section containing 27 poems have 11 poems written by members of the compiler's own clan--the Fujiwaras.

This poem neither has a complex scenery nor riddling wordplay and thus may be said to be roughly simple yet extremely picturesque. The cherry blossoms are in full bloom on a hill-slope located far away from the spot where the poet is; and he fears that the mist and fog may rise and hide the scene of the beautiful cherries hanging from their boughs. This poem involves to a certain extent the feeling of 'pity for transience of beauty' that is characteristic of the Japanese mentality. Though this developed due to Buddhist influence, there is no reason to ascertain Buddhist links to this poem. This may just be stated as a perfect example of *"mono no aware"*--a distinct Japanese thought.

74

A Failed Prayer

Minamoto no Toshiyori

Ukarikeru
Hito wo hatsuse no,
Yama oroshiyo

Hageshikare to wa
Inoranu mono wo.

Great Hatsuse shrine,
Is this for what I prayed to you:
Make her crueler still,
As the storms on Hase's hill?

This is truly an unfortunate affair or which Toshiyori writes in this *waka*. The beauty of this poem lies in the magnificent word-choices and the lucidity of the sarcasm that predominates the expression of frustration and disappointment in the poem. That beauty has also left a footprint on the English translation of the poems where instead of simple complaining, the poet is seen to ask the great shrine whether he had, by mistake, prayed for the misfortune that has befallen him.

Hatsuse shrine is another name for the Hasedera temple located in the Nara Prefecture of Japan. It is dedicated to the Buddha and originally belonged to the Tendai sect of Buddhism. It was a popular shrine as it lay on the pilgrimage route to Ise and lovers often visited it as did the poet Toshiyori. But is seems that the Gods did not favour him and his wish backfired. He is said to have been in love with a maiden who despise him and after his prayers at this Shrine she turned even more resistant. In his plight and extreme frustration Toshiyori is said to have written this poem.

The comparison of his lover's behavior to the storms on Hase's hill (Hase here refers to Hasedera hill on which the temple is located) deserves admiration being a novel thing in the anthology so far. We have witnessed comparison of cold behavior to the early morning moon and even to winter landscapes but the "storms of Hase's hill" indeed come as a fresh air to an old expression of a lover's plight. That way, this poem truly deserves to be a part of this selective collection and Teika deserves praise for his master compilation.

75

A Broken Promise

Fujiwara no Mototoshi

Chigiri okishi,
Sasemo ga tsuyu wo,
Inochi ni te,

Aware kotoshi no,
Aki mo inumeri.

As Sasemo plant on dew
On your promised words,
I depended with my life--in vain
But the year has passed away
And the autumn comes again.

This poem brings into our view how Buddhism fell into the iron-cage of Heian bureaucracy in Japan. Before going into the language of the poem first the background of it must be clarified.

In Heian Japan, Buddhism had spread far and wide, and this poem written as the Heian Era was coming to an end, captures the changes that the new order had brought to the serene monastic life of the Buddhist priests. Fujiwara no

Mototoshi (1060 - 1140) composed this poem as a complaint for the negligence of his son's request to the Chancellor Tadamichi (author of the next poem). Mototoshi's son, popularly known as Bishop *Kokaku* of the *'Kofukuji Temple'* wanted to be the Official Lecturer of the Buddhist text, *yuima-e* (Vimalakirti Sutra) -- a post of great honor and prestige. But the Chancellor paid no heed to this request and ignored it time and again.

As a result, Kokaku probably asked his father to compose this poem complaining about this negligence and possibly sent it to the Chancellor.

Here, we find a curious allegory. Mototoshi says that he (or perhaps his son) depended upon the Chancellor's promise like a 'Sasemo' plant on dew. This is intriguing because we have already encountered Sasemo plants in poem 51(The Burning Fire-Plant) only under a different name. *Sasemo* is merely another way of writing *sashimo* (in modern Japanese *Yomogi* plant) which is the Japanese Mugwort from the former poem. Though there the comparison is with the burning of the plant (a relation to fire), here it is used in relation with dew (i.e. Water). It is interesting to see how images are interchanged depending on the requirement and the poet's state of mind.

The importance of this poem to a Historian is that this poem captures the bureaucracy of the Buddhist organization of the time. Instead of the simple life that Buddha preached in India, a thousand years later, in Japan, the *Sangha* became a most complicated and structured institution. There were official lecturers of certain scriptures (as this poem relates) and they delivered lectures on them on certain occasions. However, merely having knowledge and skill was not enough to be appointed a lecturer, one also needed good family ties and support on the nobility to reach the extremely competitive and honorable position. It seems that all religious institutions, whatever their teachings ultimately succumb to "the iron-cage of Bureaucracy."

This poem actually refers to another poem attributed to Kannon, the Buddhist figurine of compassion which explains the reference of the Sasemo plants. The poem is as follows:

Nao tanome,	Translated as:	Still rely on me,
Shimeji ga hara no,		For I will help those of
Sasemo-gusa		this world for as long
Wa ga yo no naka ni,		as there are Sasemo plants
Aramu kagiri wa		in the fields of Shimeji.

76

The Blue and the Blue

Fujiwara no Tadamichi

Wata no hara,
Kogi idete mireba,
Hisakata no

Kumoi ni mayou,
Okitsu shiranami.

Sailing o'er the Sea,
I look at the distant waves,
From my ship they seem as if
The shining azure sky
And the clouds that drift along.

Fujiwara no Tadamichi--the recipient of the previous poem was the Chancellor in his time; in the anthology the name of the poet is mentioned as: "*Hoshoji no Nyudo Kanpaku Dajodaijin*" which refers to Fujiwara no Tadamichi (1097 - 1164). Thus with this poem we enter deep into the twelfth century and marks the beginning of the downfall of the Monarch and establishment of the *Samurai*-centered administration.

This poem is simple at first reading but there is something more in this poem than what appears to be. Actually, in the Imperial Court, a poem was praised entirely for its great array of meanings, its tricky word-plays, its word-usage and lastly for the imagery that it presented. So, it is natural for these poems to have multiple meanings which usurped the centre of attention of the poet while composing the poetry.

This poem through simply describes a scene that Tadamichi might have seen from his ship or boat sailing over the seas, it also uses several metaphors as well as *utamakura(s)* or pillow words. For example, the phrase *"wata no hara"* may stand for "white field of cotton" but here it qualifies to mean the sky. Again, *"okitsu shiranami"* is the pillow word used here to denote the white waves off the shore. Other pillow words used include *Hisakata* (already found in poem 33).

The comparison to the clouds to this utterly desolate imagery of the mid-ocean can be seen in a metaphorical sense, reading the clouds to mean "heaven" in the Confucian sense and thereby, drawing a relation to the emperor. In that case, the net meaning conveyed is that, the poet is becoming confused seeing the political scenario of his time. Here we must remember that the poet of this poem, Tadamichi, had an active political career during which he got badly involved in the infamous Hogen Rebellion (1156) which ultimately brought down the Emperor to being a mere puppet in the Samurai dominated system referred to before. So this makes it even more obvious for the latter interpretation to be true and thus the marks this poem as a turning point in our historical journey that we are undertaking through the poems of this anthology.

77

The Ways Part

Retired Emperor Sutoku

Se wo hayami,
Iwa ni Sekaruru,
Takigawa no

Warete mo sue ni,
Awan to zo omoi.

A boulder parts the flow
Of the river flowing swift
But I know, as it flows down
Again will they meet.

Retired Emperor Sutoku. Involved in the succession dispute resulting in th Hogen Rebellion against Tadamichi and ultimately exiled to Sanuki Island to a monastic life had a long reign and achievements worth mentioning. But this poem marks the beginning of a period of melancholic gloomy poems that are included in the anthology. This was, to a certain degree, obvious. Since the poetry of the time that are include in these official anthologies were mainly composed in the Imperial Court, the court's downfall is directly reflected in them. They often speak about the lost splendor of the court and the grandeur of the bygone days either directly, or metaphorically.

This poem directly does not capture that essence but may hint to it in metaphorical ways. This poem is believed to be on the parting of lovers and the Emperor wishes that they might meet again; somewhere, someday. This wish may also be transferred to become the emperor's wish to return to his capital from the far off Shikoku islands where he was banished to; if not a wish to regain his throne.

Just like this, most of the poems henceforth describe the lost splendor of the Heian period and perhaps the champion of that expression is the last poem by Emperor Juntoku. These poems present a sense of being lost, of losing and of sorrow and melancholy and are incomparable to those of the early parts of the anthology written about four centuries ago now. In this way the Hyakunin Isshu really becomes a historical ballad capturing Japanese history. Whether Teika foresaw it or not is perhaps irrelevant to the modern reader.

78

The Winter is Dawning Swift

Minamoto no Kanemasa

Awaji shima,
Kayou chidori no,
Naku koe ni,

Ikuyo nezamenu
Suma no sekimori.

Oh! Keepers of the Suma Gate,
How many nights have you
Been awaken by the tender cries
Of Awaji's plovers flying through.

The Japanese people have always been mesmerized by the seasons and images of natural beauty. They have involved Nature in their everyday life perhaps more than any other culture on the globe. The seasons, a most beautiful and ever-changing element of nature has been captured in the Japanese minds in more than a thousand ways. They have assigned trees and flowers to the months, and they have assigned birds to the seasons just as this poem portrays.

This poem apparently has no relation to the melancholy that is expected from the poems of this part of the anthology. But when the reader goes down to the technicalities of it, one realized that this is no different from that essence of desolation.

Awaji, is a famous island located in Japan's inland seas but for the time when this poem was composed, it was a very far-off province and from thence, plovers are flying towards the Suma gate--that is the main context of the poem. "*Chidori*" meaning "plovers" here are a typical symbol of winter in Japanese culture. The plovers are approaching the Suma gate here in a way refers to winters swift approach to the island on silent wings. And knowing the imagery which winter stood for in Japan -- the death and the desolation (poem) one must have no difficulty in drawing the connection between this poem and that melancholy spoken of before.

This poem can also be interpreted in a different way taking the meaning of the pillow-word "*chi-dori*" in the literal sense in which case it would mean "a thousand bird" -- a powerful imagery. But a thousand birds flying towards Suma gate does not complete the meaning of the poem as beautifully as reading the word to mean plover birds can and so I have retained the former meaning in my rendering of the poem. This poem has a certain reference to the Tale of Genji where the hero of the story, Genji was banished to the Suma island.

Just like plovers are accepted as the symbol of Winter in Japanese culture, other seasons also have birds assigned to them. The Japanese bush-warbler (*Uguisu*) is associated with Spring and the Lesser Cuckoo (*Hototogisu*) is associated with Summer (we will shortly encounter it in the 81st poem). Similarly wild geese (*Kari*) are associated with Summer, and this is frequently found in the Pillow Book of Sei Shonagon proving the antiquity of these relations.

Chidori(s) flying in great numbers at night from the far-off provinces bring to the mind the essence of winter's arrival and the desolation which creeps in after Autumn as well as after the Heian period, both of which are to end shortly.

79

The Light Will Find its Way

Fujiwara no Akisuke

Akikaze ni,
Tanabiku kumo no,
Taema yori

More izuru
Kage no sayakesa.

Behold the stream of moonlight
Finding its way through these,
Gracefully riven clouds
That float in the autumn breeze.

This is another poem mentioning the moon. In a way the reader often finds a certain relation between this poem and the one by Emperor Sanjo (poem 68) but the relation is similarity is merely of the tone and mood and not of any other sense.

This poem is quite different from the rest of the poems in the anthology. This is one with no allusions or metaphors. This is a very simple poem that just describes the moonlight shining through the "gracefully riven clouds". This is however, a novel imagery in the Ogura Hyakunin Isshu, for though we have encountered the moon in several poems before. The moonlight has seldom been associated with the clouds in the sky. This is actually a reference to the confounding politics of the time when the poet is gazing as the Moon and finding it surrounded with clouds. But the light is finding its way through. Thereby we understand that the poet is still hopeful and hoped that the light will always find its way through the elements that stop its progress.

But even without the allusion, the imagery is surely picturesque. The autumn (often associated with gentle evening breeze) wind is blowing and the poet is gazing at the hazy moon and the moonlit surrounding. Perhaps this captivating imagery is solely responsible for the composition of this poem, by bringing out the poetic nature from deep within the poet's heart. So, in that sense, this scenery demanded this poem. Free from allusions and need for complex analysis, this poem is a masterpiece in itself.

80

My Thoughts are In a Tangle

Lady Horikawa

Nagakaran,
Kokoro mo shirazu,
Kurokami no

Midarete kesa wo,
Mono wo koso omoe

"Do you hope forever,
Our passionate love will last?"
He answered not to me. But,
My thoughts and flowing hair
Are already in a tangle.

This poem as well does not deal with the political
confusion all around. But it is no less melancholic.
In fact, the typical imagery of entangled hair is used to
magnify that sense of confusion and distress that in this
case is entirely personal and not political as the other
poems. It is a simple, but graceful poem. Graceful because it
brilliantly depicts the sense of confusion through the image

of the disheveled hair--an instrument used very commonly be women or in poems writing about women.

The poet of the poem, Lady Horikawa served in the court of Empress Taiken who was the consort of Emperor Toba and later the mother of Emperor Sutoku. This poem is basically a *Kinuginu no uta* -- which is, if the reader remembers a Morning After poem. These poems were composed after secret lovers parted after a nocturnal meeting and sent a poem recollecting their feelings to each other. Such poems were of high importance in the Heian society around the Court and the art of writing perfect such poems was heavily praised. These also decided the course of the rest of the relationship, just as this one clearly shows.

Through asking herself the question "Does he hope: Forever / Our passionate love will last?" the poet is actually wanting to know it from the man himself about the future of their relationship. It is a witty bit of word-play and an interesting instrument for new lovers. His reply will decide her hopes, her thoughts and her future and thus she says that they are all in a tangle; which means that they are all confused and will remain so, until the reply arrives at her doorstep.

81

The Spring Has Passed

Fujiwara no Sanesada

Hototogisu,
Nakitsuru kata wo,
Nagamureba,

Tada ariake no,
Tsuki no nokoreru.

When I turned to see from where,
The cuckoo bird had cooed,
I found nothing but
The moon of early dawn.

Such a beautiful poem almost seems to jump out of the pages of the anthology and for a moment transform into a real, personal experience in itself. Such is the power of these short, four-line poems composed about a thousand years ago.

According to Professor Joshua S. Mostow, this poem was composed on the topic of "staying awake all night to hear one cry." An interesting point to note is how the coming of the season (summer) without directly mentioning it even for once. Here, the poet uses the representative bird to do the job. He writes of the "Lesser Cuckoo" or the *Hototogisu* which was characteristic of the Summer in Japanese culture. The hototogisu has cooed and the poet has turned to see from whence the sound had come and he sees the pale moon in the sky turning paler with the rising sun.

The pale moon actually hints to the brightening of the day which may stand to mean the arriving of Summer. Actually, the first call of the hototogisu is symbolic of the first arrival of summer and growing daylight signifies the dawning of summer over the land. It is most interesting to observe how the poet has mixed the two images together. He accomplishes the deed by letting one of them remain unfinished and hanging in mid-air--the cuckoo bird is only heard, not seen. Just as summer's approach cannot be literally seen. These are the trifles of poetic imagination that really move us and make us connect to the days in which this poem was composed--about nine centuries ago.

The term used here to mean the moon--"*Ariake*" is a special term for the moon of the early dawn or daybreak. It is usually associated with coldness and parting in Japanese poetry just as here it is used to signify the coldness of Winter which is fading away with the rising sun of summer. A marvelous way to depict the transformation of seasons--a most dominant phenomenon in the Temperate Zone and particularly Japan.

82

A Cruel Blow

Fujiwara no Atsuyori

Omoi wabi,
Satemo inochi wa,
Aru mono wo,

Uki ni taenu wa,
Namida nari keri.

Though in deep anguish
I've survived your cruel blow,
In grief I could not check this flood,
And now my tears-- will flow.

The author of this poem, Atsuyori became a Buddhist monk in 1172 and came to be known as [Dhamma-Master] Doin. Though crucial for interpretation, there in, as of yet, no way of knowing if this poem was composed before or after taking tonsure for in either cases, this might have different meanings behind it.

This type of poems are generally contextual and thus, knowing the context and setting is crucial for understanding them. Astuyori is said to have frequently attended poetry competitions and had a collection of poems for himself, but unfortunately nothing of that survives and we do not even know if this poem was written after being hurt by a cruel lover or casually in a poetry competition.

If is was written before he took tonsure, then this might have some personal and literal background. Perhaps the poet was hurt by a lover or betrayed by a trusted man. But after taking to Buddhism, he might write this in a more metaphysical sense when this might be aimed at life itself. He might be contemplating his life as a worldly-man and speaking about the blow that life had meted out to him, which might well be the reason for taking tonsure at all.

Anyhow, this poem again captures that gloom and sorrow that had crept into the psyche of the men attached to the Heian court who were pained to witness its downfall in the post-Hogen Rebellion days. The following poem is also by a court noble and captures a similar essence of a cruel blow and a desire to escape.

83

There is No Escape

Fujiwara no Toshinari

Yo no naku yo,
Michi koso nakere,
Omoi iru,

Yama no oku ni mo,
Shika zo naku naru.

Is there truly nowhere
Where I may escape to?
Even in these mountain depths
I hear the deer's cry.

F ujiwara no Toshinari is one of the most important
figures in the anthology. The reason is that he was the
father of the compiler of the anthology Fujiwara no Teika.
Not only did he have immense influence of his son, but also
was one of the most influential men in the poetry circles of
his time. There were a large number of students (authors of
poems numbered 81, 86 and 87) who were associated with
him and a large number of poets were also his students
of poetry (poem no. 89, 98) but then again, certain poets

such as Fujiwara no Akisuke (poem 79) were fiercely in opposition to him. Anyhow, his importance in the poetry circles of his day is quite clear from these references.

This poem again brings to our mind the melancholy and the nostalgia that the poet is facing probably as he is reminded of the past splendor of the Heian court. He witnesses the change in society and is left with no choice but to resort to escapism. He wants to escape from the society and deciding to do so, he has entered the pristine forests away from human madness and politics. But even here, the deer's cry invoked the same essence of melancholy and sadness that he vehemently tried to bury deep in his heart. This is however, only a general and one-sided interpretation of this poem. There is another school of scholars who believe that this poem has nothing to do with the state of society of that point of time and it was the thought of his mortality that pushed him to compose such a poem.

In regard of the latter, I would like to draw a parallel with the fifth poem in this anthology-- "The Wandering Stag" by Sarumaru Dayu which also involves feelings of *memento mori* (reminder of death) and draws the imagery of the crying stag treading the path laid with autumn leaves. Whether the Stag signifies this feeling of mortality in Japanese culture is not known to me, but it is intriguing how things link up in the Hyakunin Isshu be it poets or images--though composed over four centuries they exhibit an unbroken stream of expression more like a ballad than an anthology.

Coming to the technical parts of the poem. There are a few intelligent pivot words with double-meanings. As Professor Mostow explains, the word in the third line, "*omoi iru*" may mean "to set one's heart upon" but again, "*iru*" means "to enter". Actually, both the meanings are supposed to be taken into account when translating it, but for the sake of the poetic essence, I have left out the first part of the meaning which is beautifully included in Professor Mostow's translation which I quote underneath:

> Within this world
> there is, indeed, no path!
> Even deep in this mountains
> I have entered, heart set,
> I seem to hear the deer cry!

--From the "Pictures of the Heart:
The Hyakunin Isshu in Word and Image"

By Prof. J. S. Mostow

84

Nostalgia

Fujiwara no Kiyosuke

Nagaraeba,
Mata kono koro ya,
Shinobaren

Ushi to mishi yo zo
Ima wa koishiki.

If I should live longer,
By the memory lane
Will these days there be?
For days I once thought of as dark,
I find now dear to me.

On the surface, this appears to be a simple poem on nostalgia. How bitter experiences later appear as cherished memories. In a sense this may actually draw from Kiyosuke's own life. When speaking of Kiyosuke, we must remember that he had a bitter disagreement with his father regarding poetry and ended up establishing the *Rokujo* School of poetry after that. It is interesting to note that the father of Kiyosuke was none other that the poet of the 79th poem--Akisuke.

This poem is simple and uses no word-plays or complicated imagery worth describing. So I leave the interpretation of the poem to the reader who will find it easy to relate to their personal experiences.

What is worth mentioning regarding this poem is the mood. The reference to the dark days is in a way a repetition of the reference of melancholia that is creeping into the Japanese psyche of that time. What Kiyosuke thinks is that although the times in which he is living are dark he hopes that they will lighten up and appear as cherished memories "dear" to him in the future just like the memories of the past dark times are now appearing to be.

Perhaps this is a lighter way of looking at the darkness of the changing times. Then the Japanese to not appear to be so morose a people as they are often accused of being.

85

I Spend my Hours of Darkness

Dhamma-Master Shun'e

Yo mo sugara,
Mono omou koro wa,
Ake yaranu,

Nae no hima sae,
Tsure nakari keri.

All these sleepless nights,
I drag through longing hours
But these heartless bedroom shutters
Keep the light from me.

A Buddhist monk, the poet. But what is to be praised is his capacity to marvelously express the feelings of a young girl in his poetry. This was a typical requirement of Japanese poetry-competitions in the Heian period. The bedroom shutters here symbolize her doorway to the rest of the world and to her lover. They are heartless because they do not light up early and even longer seems the night. We can draw a parallel with poem numbered 3 by Hitomaro and this poem. Both depict a sense of longing. But there

231

is a fundamental difference in the two poems. While the former was written portraying a genuine feeling of being dragged through life, this was composed in a poetry competition which makes its feelings, not necessarily, but usually imaginary. Thus the author might never have felt the emotion that he is found to write about in his poem though his expertise and the beauty of the poem lies in the flawless expression of that emotion.

86

Oh! When I See the Moon

Dhamma-Master Saigyo

Nageke tote,
Tsuki ya wa mono wo,
Omowasuru,

Kakochi gao naru
Waga nami dakana.

Should the Moon be blamed
For inviting this sadness?
When I lift my gloomy face,
I know my tears are flowing.

Dhamma-Master Saigyo had an interesting career whilst in the capital as Sato no Narikiyo. He was a promising nobleman and had a great fortune to inherit drawing the attention of both Emperor Toba and Emperor Sutoku. But despising the complicating politics of the capital he chose to abandon it and took the life of a wandering mendicant. He took tonsure, adopted the name "Saigyo" and started living in the mountain-monastery of *Koyasan*. Years later, he returned to the capital and found it entirely changed by the Hogen Rebellion, the Emperor Sutoku banished in Shikoku and Kiyomori ruling as a warlord (after a few years, his entire clan will be wiped out in the Genpei War). Despising this state of affairs, Saigyo again took to roaming about while the Samurai-led government of the Kamakura period established its sway over the land. Saigyo traveled and composed poems lamenting the loss and death of his contemporaries and the loss of the Heian splendor. This poem may also be taken to express such a context in a way. He is seeing the moon and is lamenting the changed in the political sphere. After all, the Moon has often been "blamed" for the invocation of nostalgia in more than one culture.

This poem is said to have been influenced by he poems of a famous Chinese poet named *Bo Juyi*. I believe that the poem which may be though to the the inspiration for this one is the *"Cheng-hen-ge"* or "The Song of Everlasting Regret" by Bo Juyi composed during the T'ang Period. We must remember that the T'ang Period of China had immense influence in shaping the Heian period of Japan and so this relation may not be illogical.

Some say that this poem expresses the feelings of a resentful lover. But perhaps simply gazing at the moon, brings forth this kind of a sadness.

87

The Mist is Rising

Dhamma-Master Jakuren

Murasame no,
Tsuyu mo made hinu,
Maki no ha ni,

Kiri tachinoboru,
Aki no yugure.

The dusk of autumn sets,
And the mist on the valley cleaves.
But the droplets, of the passing rain,
Still rest on Fir-tree leaves.

This poem, otherwise would never have drawn any attention if it wasn't composed by the nephew of Teika's father. Jakuren's name before taking tonsure was Fujiwara no Sadanaga and he was counted as a leading poet of the house of *Mikohidari*. It is said that Jakuren was asked to aid in the compilation of the Shin-Kokinshu but he died before the task was completed. This poem, was initially not praised by Teika and was made the cutting-floor of the anthology that he compiled. But this poem suddenly springs up among the very carefully selected poems of the Hyakunin Isshu compiled by his relative. This is in fact strange and surprising that Teika should have a change of mind and include it in one of his most important works.

The primary accusation behind denouncing this poem initially was its simplicity. Most scholars believe it to be a simple descriptive poem capturing the scenery of an autumn dusk. But the very fact that it speaks of autumn makes it even more intriguing and drives us to draw a relation to winter's arrival. And the feeling of retreating warmth at winter's arrival can very well be paralleled with the feeling of nostalgia that moves the poets of this period eulogizing the bygone splendor. Although it was not worthy of praise according to Teika's evaluation based on the measures of his time, this poem is in itself a masterpiece from the modern perspective.

Professor Mostow points out that the phrase *"kiri tachinoboru"* meaning "the mist is now rising" used frequently by later poets was actually coined by Jakuren in this poem.

This same poem is also found in the Shin-Kokin-Wakashu as poem numbered 491 under the section entitles "Autumn".

88

As Short as the Reeds that Grow

Lady Betto

Naniwa-e no,
Ashi no karine no
Hitoyo yue,

Mi wo tsukushite ya,
Koi wataru beki.

After sleeping this night,
As short as a piece of reeds
that grow on Naniwa Bay
Must I long and wait for him
Till I'm blown away.

Naniwa Bay again surfaces in this poem. Previously, it has been mentioned in poems numbered 19 and 20 and also finds mention in the famous poem in the Kokin-Wakashu given at the beginning of the anthology (Pg. 01) composed by the semi-legendary poet-scholar Wani. As for the poet, Lady Betto is known to be the daughter of Minamoto no Yoshitaka and served in the circles of Empress Seishi who was Emperor Sutoku's wife.

The imagery of this poem is traditional. For some, reason, the poet knows that it is for the last time that she is meeting her lover and that the present meeting is their last meeting. She is shivering at the fact that she will have to pine and wait for him for the rest of her life.I have used the word "blown" in the last line of the English version of the poem. The actual meaning in this case is she fears that she will have to wait till she is beyond this mortal world. I would like to mention here that since I am bringing the essence of shivering from fear,

This poem contains a large number of word-plays that make this a truly remarkable one. Such as, the word "*karine*" may either mean "to cut at the root" implying cut pieces of the reeds, as well as, "a short nap". But as the reader by now must be aware that the meaning conveyed retains both the meanings. Again, "*hitoyo*" may mean a single segment of a reed as well as, a single night; again the conveyed meaning is: 'a night as short as a segment of a reed.' Similarly, "*mi wo tsukushi*" may mean either 'to exhaust oneself' as well as, the famous channel-markers of Osaka (found in poem 20).

Although Lady Betto is an unknown poet, she seems to have been greatly talented in poetry compositions. Who knows how many other such talented poets never found their way to the imperial anthologies and forever remained in the dark spheres outside the court.

89

Oh! Jeweled String, My Life

Shokushi Naishinno

Tama no o yo,
Taenaba taene,
Nagaraeba

Shinoburu koto no,
Yowari mo zo suru.

My power to hide this love,
Will but weaken still
Oh! Jeweled string--my life
If you break; you must break now.

The poet, Shokushi Naishinno, is actually the daughter of the Emperor Go-Shirakawa and was appointed the high priestess of the Kamo Shrine near Kyoto. The Kamo shrine was considered important for the security of the imperial capital and thus its high priestess had to be the daughter of the reigning Emperor. Usually she was appointed following her father's coronation and removed as a new emperor ascended the throne. During this period she was supposed to be a vestal virgin as is already mentioned in the commentary of the 63rd poem by Michimasa. Thus she was not supposed to have affairs with men and her activities were strictly guided by rules.

This poem was composed, probably in a poetry competition where the assigned subject was "hidden love". It is beautiful how she could express the feeling of being burdened by hidden love, although she never likely experienced it. Or perhaps the feeling that she was expressing was true and this poem is similar to the poem by Michimasa (poem 63). Maybe she could not express her love because of the rules of her office.

Anyhow, the imagery used to express the burden is beautiful and witty. She compares her life to a string. A string holding that secrecy. And she is now feeling that secret is overwhelming her and that string binding it is about to break. She then wants it to break that very moment instead of later, when it might be too late.

90

I Would Like To Show Him

Inpu Moin no Taiyu

Misebaya na
Ojima no ama no
Sode dani mo

Nure ni zo nureshi
Iro wa kawarazu

I'd like to show him these--
On Ojima's shores,
Even the fishermen's sleeves are wet,
But when they wet, they're wet indeed
And do not change their shade.

This is a very intriguing poem among the large bouquet of simple images. But that is what makes it even more beautiful. It stands out like a solitary blossom among a great multitude of commonplace flowers. The poet of this verse, Inpu Moin no Taiyu served in the circles of Princess Ryoshi, the daughter of Go-shirakawa. (Ryoshi was known as Inpumo-In ans hence the naming). She was a very accomplished and capable poet and was a member of the "Garden of Poetic Flowers." According to the headnote, this poem was composed in a poetry competition and the assigned topic was "Love."

In reality, this poem is a poetic variation of a similar poem composed a few centuries ago composed by Minamoto no Shigeyuki (see poem 48) and found in the Go-Shuishu as numbered 4: 828. The poem is as follows:

Matsushima ya,	Translated as:	Ah! Matsushima,
Wojima no iso ni,		the sleeves of the fishermen
Asari seshi,		who fish of the beach,
Ama no sode koso		of Male isle must be soaked
Kaku ho nureshika		like the tear-soaked sleeves of mine.

--Courtesy: Prof. J. S. Mostow

Professor Mostow explains that the reference to "he" in the poem by Taiyu is actually Shigeyuki. The poem is interesting because it has a reference to the colloquial saying that if those fisherman's sleeves are wet, mine are red with blood-red tears. Reference to sleeves wet by tears have been found in poems 42, 65 ans 72 earlier. So the poet also alludes to this saying and this poem combining the two to convey her thought that she wants to show Shigeyuki that is he thinks that only the fishemen's sleeves are wet, he is wrong and her sleeves are wet by bloody tears that have changed the shade of the sleeves.

Male Island is one of the hundreds of little isles in the island-chain of Matsushima in the modern Miyagi Prefecture.

91

The Loneliness of Night

Fujiwara no Yoshitsune

Kirigirisu,
Naku ya shimoyo no,
Sa mushiro ni,

Koromo katashiki
Hitori kamo nen.

On this frosty winter night,
Alone must I lie?
While through this darkness rings,
The lonely cricket's cry.

This poem would ideally be befitting of a Buddhist monk. But, Fujiwara no Yoshitsune was a poet of great fame and belonged to the elite poetry house of Mikohidari and was the grandson of Jien (poem 95). He was among the editors of the Shin Kokin-Wakashu.

This poem is in a way similar to the third poem in the anthology by Hitomaro. It is interesting to note how repetitive poems are appearing in the closing poems of the anthology. Moreover, the load of inter-textual content has also increased. There is a poem in the Shin Kokin-Wakashu that is closely related to this poem. Anyhow, this poem has a certain degree of novelty in it--the crickets come as a gust of fresh air among the repetitive imagery if the poem. But to the more romantic readers this poem is a masterpiece, not only does it invoke the beauty of the dead night--the sound of silence is also captured remarkably in here.

Coming to the technicalities of the poem, the poem that this poem refers to (acting as the foundation poem or *honka*) is found in the Shin Kokin-Wakashu numbered 4: 689. It is as follows:

Sa-mushiro ni,	Translated as:	On the cold reed mat,
Koromo kata shiki		spreading out her robe just for once
Kiyohi mo ya		this evening too,
Ware mo matsuramu		is she waiting for me
Ujhi no hashi-hime		the Goddess of Uji Bridge?

Courtesy: Prof. J. S. Mostow

Now if one notices, one will see that the first two lines of this poem and the third and fourth lines of Yoshitsune's poem are identical. Again if the reader turns to the third poem in this anthology by Hitomaro, he will notice that the last lines of Hitomaro's and the Yoshitsune's poems are again the same. These similarities cannot be entirely claimed to be copying or imitations. Yoshitsune is more like quoting or paying homage to the poets of ancient days and this was an accepted and highly revered practice among the poetry circles of Heian Japan. And as professor Mostow points out, the *honka(s)* were never mentioned, the poems were actually meant for an educated audience who were supposed to be well versed in the classics (Hitomaro's poem, by Yoshitsune's times had attained classical status).

Actually, this poem has a beautiful contrast of colours. It speaks of snow which is white and the night-time, which is black in colour. Altogether, the inclusion of the crickets truly make this a wonderful piece of poetry.

92

My Sleeves are Wet

Nijo-In no Sanuki

Wa ga sode wa,
Shiohi ni mienu,
Oki no ishi no,

Hi koso shirane,
Kawaku mamo nashi.

Like the hidden rocks at sea,
Unseen even at ebb-tide,
So are the sleeves of mine--
No one knows of them, yet,
Not a moment they are dry.

Sanuki was a leading poet of her time though the exact dates of her life her unknown. She served the retired Emperor Nijo and a number of poems are attributed to her.

This poem uses the old imagery of sleeves getting get. This same topic has bee found recurrently throughout the Hyakunin Isshu and were very popular topics in poetry competitions. However, although this is the fifth poem on this topic in this anthology, the degree of novelty added by Sanuki truly makes it stand apart from the others. An important feature of this age is the experimentation that we are witnessing in the poems. The poets are using more uncommon and hitherto unseen images usually in the form of accompaniments to bring out the feeling. This poem is uses the imagery of the rocks submerged by the sea which are always wet, but never seen by the men above. She uses this image to compare it to her sleeves as well as to show her desperation.

This poem has an interesting parallel to the 48th poem in the anthology "The Lashing Waves" by Minamoto no Shigeyuki mentioning the feeling of being lashed onto the shore by the turbulent waves. Perhaps it had also influenced this poem, but after all, the *honka(s)* were never meant to be mentioned but understood.

Now, it is queer to note, that later poets and scholars have referred to Sanuki as *"oki no ishi no Sanuki"*. So it seems that her reputation had received a major boost after this poem and she became famous principally because of it. Another instance of such exemplary incident is the poet Kunaikyo being called *"wakakusa no Kunaikyo"* (*"wakakusa"* means young herbs) after a famous verse she wrote (included in the Shin Kokin-Wakashu) which is the following poem:

> Light and dark,
> The green of the field's
> Young herbs,
> Distinct
> In patches of fading snow.

Courtesy: Prof. J. S. Mostow

So it seems that just as a single poem could ruin one's career in the court as we have seen earlier, it could also uplift one's status to near immorality. It only exemplifies the importance of poetry in the Heian court and society.

93

The Fishing Boats

Minamoto no Sanetomo

Yo no naka wa,
Tsune ni mo ga mo na.
Nagisa kogu

Ama no obune no,
Tsuna de kanashi mo.

If the worlds would remain,
Unmoved as it is.
How marvelous is the sight
Of the long ropes towing
The fishing boats to shore!

It seems that the melancholy of the age did not even spare the new people in power. To understand this poem, first one must understand the life and times of Sanetomo. Before, going into his political life, I think it would be worthwhile to mention, that he studied poetry under the compiler Fujiwara no Teika himself and a high standard of poetry is thus expected of him. Minamoto no Sanetomo was not only a nobleman, but the third *Shogun* of the newly established Kamakura shogunate. The country was then still recovering from the horrors of the war and the seat of absolute power had shifted from Heian-kyo to the eastern city of Kamakura. Sanetomo, in spite of being the Shogun was not at peace, he knew that his relatives were plotting against him and he almost became paranoid from that fear. However, as future events would prove, his fears were not entirely baseless; he was assassinated by his cousin at the age of 28 at the *Tsurugaoka Hachimangu* shrine in 1219 CE. It shows how weak the new centre of power was and the troubled soul of the new *shogun* truly deserves to be pitied.

It is from this mentality that this poem is written. Sanetomo wishes that the world to remain the same without any change (maybe he is also regretting the change that has already come about in the political structure of the state.) then we sees the scene of the fishing boats being drawn back to harbour. He feels calm and it soothes his being. This poem is thus an expression of timelessness. Sanetomo is feeling that though the times through which he is living are terrible, those boats and their world has never changed and he is overcome by a desire for being a part of this. This is truly a masterpiece in this regard.

94

The Ancient Capital

Sangi Fujiwara no Masatsune

Miyoshino no,
Yama no aki-kaze,
Sayo fukete,

Furusato samuku
Koromo utsu nari.

An autumn winds blow
From Mount Yoshino's slopes
Deepening the night, so clear.
While the ancient capital shivers,
The fulling of cloths I hear.

This poem marvelously relates to two other poems of this anthology--the 31st and 98th poem in its context. Fujiwara no Masatsune, was an accomplished poet and one of the editors of the Shin Kokin-Wakashu. He also established the Asukai school of poetry and studied poetry under Shunzei.

The common reader might not be aware of the term "fulling of cloth". It is an old practice which is called

"*Koromo utsu*" in Japan. In the process, usually woolen textiles are placed on a wood or stone surface and beaten with a wooden mallet. It is done to improve the texture as well as to give it a glossy appearance. The sound of it, the poet considers a typical heralding symbol for winter when those woolen textiles will be required.

This poem uses certain interesting scenes to churn the feeling of autumn in the hearts of the readers. He brings the image of the wind blowing from Yoshino's slopes (Yoshino's snow is referred to in the 31st poem); and clearly uses the word "autumn wind" (*aki-kaze*). Then he brings the context of clear nights. Autumn nights are usually described to be calm and clear all around the world. Again, he writes that *furusato* or the ancient capital Nara is shivering from the autumn winds and dew and with the picture of a "deepening" autumn night the scene is complete. The deepening is both the deepening of the Winter as well as the night.

The use of the term *furusato* is intriguing. Literally, "*furusato*" means Hometown. But here the ancient capital- -Nara is being referred to as *furusato*. It is actually because, even after the capital was changed to Heian-kyo or Kyoto in 794 CE, poets and scholars continued to call it a "hometown", or the "ancient capital" or even the "ancient throne" (poem 61) with a certain essence of nostalgia related with it. After all, we must remember that it was at Nara that the Japanese culture received its largest boot that was instrumental to its flowering in the Heian period. During the Nara period, Japanese culture received an admixture of Chinese art and poetry, Indian Buddhism and developed its own distinct style in the years that followed.

95

I Hide This World of Tears

Former Archbishop Jien

Okenaku
Ukiyo no tami ni
Ou kana

Waga tatsu soma ni
Sumizome no sode

From my mountain monastery,
Set in the lonely timber-woods.
This world of tears I see, and pine.
I try but fail, to shield it with
These ink-black sleeves of mine.

This is the last of the poems written by Buddhist monks in this anthology. He was a monk of the Tendai sect that started gaining popularity from the Heian period. Moreover, he was the son of Tadamichi(poem 76) and the nephew of Yoshitsune (poem 91) and Teika himself. Thus, we had sufficient family ties to be be given this important status. But we must not undermine his poetry in the end.

This poem is composed entirely from the Buddhist point-of-view which makes it difficult to ascertain whether it was composed for a competition or for personal reflection. Anyhow, this poem laments the darkness of the world and the poet seems to assume the mentality of a Bodhisattva. Bodhisattva are those worldly creatures that have attained Buddhahood (Bodhi) but have an outward approach towards the world and remain in here to help other creatures come out of this "world of tears." Thus he claims that he is trying to shield the world with his sleeves but in vain. The Buddhist world-view is predominantly transient and full of suffering. So the reference to the "world of tears" is very apt here however, Professor Mostow suspects that there is an allusion to Emperor Daigo here who is said to have been very compassionate (like a Bodhisattva). It is said that once he had taken off his robes of a cold winter night to experience the same pain as his subjects. But that being unclear, we will go on with the general interpretation of the poem.

One interesting point in this poem is that the fourth line of the poem is a direct quotation of the words of the founder of the Tendai sect in Japan--Saicho he used the words *"waga tatsu soma ni"* meaning, "in these timber woods that I enter" in a famous *waka* composed on Mount Hiei (quoted below). Due to this relation, many medieval commentators had believed that this poem was composed by Jien quite like a vow to adhere by the Tendai sect when he became the chief-abbot of Mount Hiei in 1192; but this view is untenable (because this poem is also found in another anthology *"Senzaishu"* compiled in 1188). Another point to note is the use of the word "ink-black sleeves". The word *"sumizome"* in Japanese means "black as ink" (*sumi* being the Japanese ink). It emphasizes his Buddhist identity and authority to a great extent; black being the colour of the robes worn by the Buddhist monks in East Asia like red is worn in Tibet. As mentioned earlier, all through the poem, the identity and consciousness of the poet at being a Buddhist monk is very strong in this poem and finds place in the message that he tries to deliver through it. He wants to shield himself as well as the world from this pain of the "world of tears" but his ink-black sleeves prove insufficient for the task.

The poem that Jien alludes to, composed by Saicho (767 - 822 CE) is as follows:

Anokutara,	Translated as:	Most omniscient
Samiyaku sabojhi		and supremely enlightened,
Hotoke-tachi		Buddha hosts,
Wa ga tatsu soma ni		On this timber forest that I enter,
Miyauga arase-tamahe		Bestow your divine protection!
		---*Shin Kokin-Wakashu* (20: 1921)
		Courtesy: Prof. J. S. Mostow

96

It is But My Age

Fujiwara no Kintsune

Hana sasou
Arashi no niwa no
Yuki nara de

Furi yuku mono wa
Waga mi nari keri

Painting my gardens gray--
Its not the snow from blossoms,
That fall in the stormy winds.
But the years of my life.
Brush my hairs white.

Fujiwara no Kintsune was one of the helpers of Teika in compiling the Hyakunin Isshu after he married Kintsune's elder sister. It is thus unlikely that his poems would not be found in the anthology. However, this poem deserves a place by its own right though. The imagery is confusing and in a certain way may qualify as a manifestation of the poetic instrument-- "elegant confusion."

The poet, Kintsune, is said to have aided in the establishment of the new sect of the Fujiwara clan--the Saionji (named after their seat-of-power, a temple to the north of Kyoto) after the Jokyu Rebellion wherein the Kamakura shogunate defeated the Emperor Gotoba and decisively marked the end of the emperor's supremacy. Around that temple, it is said, that Kintsune planted many cherry trees and dug lakes etc. beautifying the place. It is believed that this poem is written while observing the cherry blossoms being blown away by the wind near that temple. The poet sees this beautiful scene and contemplates his own life closing. This thought makes him think that this storm (incidents in life?) is scattering but the years of his life that is making his branches bare.

The poet uses a curious word here. *"Hana fubuki"*. Hana fubuki literally means a great scattering of a huge number of blossoms. Its more life snowfall and that is why the word *arashi* (storm) is used instead of the simple *kaze* meaning wind. The poet actually contemplates his own downfall from a position of great power and thus uses this phrasing for the Japanese word used in the fourth line *furi* means both "to fall" as well as, "to grow old" it is actually a pillow word used dramatically and fantastically.

Note: The ideal pillow word in thus case would have been but the one used in the 17th poem by Narihira--Chihayaburu.

97

I Burn and Burn

Fujiwara no Teika

Konu hito o
Matsuho no ura no
Yunagi ni

Yaku ya moshio no
Mi mo kogare tsutsu.

For the man who never comes,
I wait on an evening, calm--
Like sea-weed on Matsuho's shore,
My being is set afire,
And I burn for ever more.

This has to be the most important poem in the Hyakunin Isshu of Fujiwara no Teika--the compiler's own composition. All through this anthology we have witnessed the wit and poetic sense of Teika and now is our chance to witness his own poetic genius. This poem apparently is simple till the time we realize that the author has changed his perspective. It is from the view-point of a woman that he is composing this poem--one of the characteristics of the genius poet. Moreover, in this poem he refers to the original anthology of ancient Japanese literature--the Man'yoshu. The imagery of burning sea-weed is taken from a poem in that ancient anthology composed by Kasa Kanamura in ca. 726 CE (numbered 935 - 937 in Vol. 6). The interesting points of the poem gradually surface after the reader delves into the sentence and word-usage of the poem.

The image of the burning (or boiling) sea-weeds is impressive. The sea-weed is not only used to refer to the bitterness or tears but also to allude to the feeling of emptiness of tears and a feeling of burning of the body. It is actually an old Japanese tradition that Teika is alluding to. In olden days, the Japanese used brine and sea-weed to obtain salt. They were first dried and then boiled or burnt on the shore--a scene that this poem alludes to. This burning on the shore has some special significance beyond the obvious. The medieval commentaries stressed on this heavily. They say that Matsuho's Bay being located on Awaji island requires the lover to come from the other side of the sea (i.e. from Honshu) and this is supported by the use of the letter *ho* in Matsuho which means "to sail". "*Moshiyo*"(in line 4) is the burning sea-weed that has been referred to in this poem. In sum, this poem is a masterpiece in its expression according to both the Heian as well as the modern point-of-view and demands special attention being composed by the compiler himself. It is interesting to note, that commentators have claimed that speaker of this poem has been waiting for year on end but the term -*tsutsu* suggests that she has waited simply for "many nights." Interestingly, there are a lot of word-plays in this poem the word "Matsuho" contains the word "matsu" which may mean "to wait" or even "pine trees".

Lastly, Matsuo or Matsuho Bay is located on the northern tip of Awaji Isle in the Japanese inland seas. It remains to this day, a popular tourist spot.

98

And Now the Summer's Past

Fujiwara no Ietaka

Kaze soyogu
Nara no ogawa no
Yugure wa

Misogi zo natsu no
Shirushi nari keru

At Nara, the autumn whispers,
Among the trees of Oak
And the ablutions at the Little Stream
Are the only sign of summer.

Medieval as well as modern commentators disagree regarding the exact interpretation of this poem. Some seem to stress more on the rites being referred to here, while others claim the season to be the decisive imagery. Whatever it be this poem, writes about the changing of the season--an aspect of nature that has intrigued Japanese people since time immemorial.

What is enchanting about this poem is the use of the little signs and symbols that add-up to create the essence of the summer departing and the autumn setting in. This is an instrument of poetry that we have also observed in Poem 94 by Masatsune (The Ancient Capital). What novelty it adds to the old scenery is through the mentioning of the ablutions at the "Little Stream" or *Nara-no-Ogawa*. "*Misogi*", in reality a Shinto ritual that has been in vogue since antiquity and involves ritual bathing and purification in Summer.

The Japanese believe that they accumulate evil impurities through ill actions and terrifying experiences. Thus in the summer they performed this ritual purification called *mina-zuki-barae* or Six-Months-Purification. This is the picture captured in the poem but the involvement of Nara and the departing summer has some significance in this poem.

Nara, being the ancient capital, we cannot overlook the possibility of nostalgia whereby, this poem may draw heavily from Masatsune's poem (poem 94). That means, combining the two poems the meaning conveyed may be, that the splendor the the past days are gone and the "ancient capital shivers" yet there is warmth and the old traditions remain there reminding us the poet of the bygone days. However, this relation cannot be generalized for it takes the meanings or the seasons in the metaphorical sense which might not be the obvious case.

Professor Mostow notes, that there is yet another source from which this poem heavily draws from. It is from there that the poet takes the imagery of the ablutions at Nara-no-Ogawa or "Little Stream". It is found in the *Kokin Rokujo*:

Misogi suru	Translated as:	In the river's wind,
Nara no Ogawa no,		at Nara-no-Ogawa where,
Kaha kaze ni,		they purify themselves,
Inori zo wataru		"May my love, unknown to others never cease!"--
Shita ni taeji to.		That is what I keep praying for!

Courtesy: Prof. J. S. Mostow

However, in absence of directly quoted lines, these allusions remain questionable and doubtful. But that in no way reduces the beauty of and elegance of the poem by Ietaka.

99

This World is A Gloom

Emperor Gotoba

Hito mo oshi
Hito mo urameshi
Ajiki naku

Yo o omou yue ni
Mono omou mi wa.

There are men for whom I grieve,
And Men I hate to see.
With my sadness; I always feel
"This world is a gloom to me."

Emperor Gotoba (1180 - 1239) assumes prominent role in the revival of *waka* in the Imperial court during the Kamakura period. But he himself seems to have a troublesome life with many ups and downs. He commissioned Fujiwara no Teika and was instrumental to the composition of the Kokin-Wakashu and the Shin Kokin-Wakashu. However, he had certain disagreements with Teika regarding his freewheeling style of poetry and when Teika openly criticised the emperor, he got him exiled for a year which led to a distant and cold relationship with Teika for the following years. Meanwhile though, Teika got closed to Gotoba's son, Emperor Juntoku with whom he finishes the Ogura Hyakunin Isshu.

This poem is interesting because it is certainly not one of the best poems by Emperor Gotoba who was an ardent lover and patron of *waka* poetry. The reason for Teika to include this poem in the anthology is perhaps because of his detestation towards the Emperor. To understand this poem, one needs to go into the depths of his life in a general sense. Emperor Gotoba was bold enough to protest against the Kamakura supremacy. He wanted to reinstate the Imperial court at the centre of power. So he and his son, [the future Emperor] Juntoku staged a rebellion in 1221 famous as the Jokyu Disturbance where he called all the samurais to accept his subjugation. But most of them, not wanting to lose their new status sided with the Shogunate and defeated the Emperor who was banished to Oki Island (poem 11). Gotoba spent eighteen years in exile till his death in 1239.

Though it may be apparent but this poem was composed before the rebellion and exile, possibly in 1212 as a part of a series entitled "Personal Grievance".

In all, the gloomy life and sad downfall of Emperor Gotoba most likely prompted him to compose this poem more than the subject of the series. Here the poet probably alludes to the new samurai class and their associates as his foes and the men he hates "to see." However, this is not completely clear who these men are specifically. And even the emperor has left no hint towards that. He simply used the word "*hito*" meaning person or persons in his poetry. Thus this poem remains one of the mysterious yet thoughtful poems of the anthology.

100

The Day Is Past

Retired Emperor Juntoku

Momoshiki ya
Furuki nokiba no
Shinobu ni mo

Nao amari aru
Mukashi nari keri.

In this brilliant ancient house,
Along the hanging eaves,
The Shinobu grasses grow.
However many they are,
My memories are always more.

The anthology, the age, the importance of the emperor, and the Emperor himself comes to a gloomy end with this poem and contrary to Arthur Waley's claim this is perhaps the most brilliant ending that this anthology could ever have had. Emperor Juntoku was banished to the *Sado* Islands following the Jokyu Rebellion of 1221 and had a sad demise there, after spending 20 years in exile. So, this poem in a way balances out the entire anthology. Emperor

Tenji, with whom it all began was a powerful, successful and kind emperor while Emperor Juntoku, was weak and by then the Emperor was almost a vestigial organ of state operations. This anthology beautifully brings to light the changing nature of the politics and this ending completes the *metamorphosis*.

This poem was probably composed in 1216, five years before the rebellion and exile. It elegantly portrays the emperors eulogy to the splendor of the early Heian court and beautifully contrasts the bright image of the state as captured in the early parts of the anthology.

This poem, draws from another poem of the oldest anthology of Japanese verse, the Man'yoshu which contains a poem mentioning how people at the palace decorate their hairs with plum blossoms and speaks of how free and carefree, life at the palace is. The poet plays on this poem to convey the opposite meaning while he sees his ancient palace falling into desolation and dying out into darkness.

"Shinobu" is a sort of grass, a creeping vine but also symbolized nostalgia (it also means "to love"). Shinobu grass is used particularly in this imagery because the poet wants to imagine himself twining onto the palace in the same way as those creepers entwine their supports.

The use of the term *"Momoshiki"* is interesting. He takes the term from the poem in the Man'yoshu but gives it his own touch. *Momoshiki* may mean Hundred-fold palace as professor Mostow says or "Hundred. . . . . laid out" referring to the hundred mats lain out of the numerous people attending court. It may also mean "hundred stones laid out" and they all refer to the Imperial Palace or *"Kyuchu"*. It is a powerful poetic device used to allude to the fact that however powerful a house, rot affects and it ultimately declines into the same state in which he now sees his brilliant palace.

This poem brings the entire era of great poets and poetry, culture and sophistication to an end. The Ogura Hyakunin Isshu, an anthology of chronologically arranged poems which traces the flourishing of this age from the Asuka Enlightenment to its height in the tenth and eleventh centuries also end with its downfall having completed its course of a "hundred poems, by a hundred poets."

The Hundred Poets

(626 - 1242 CE)

Brief Biographical Notes

Emperor Tenchi (626 - 672)

Emperor Tenchi (or Tenji), born as Prince Naka no Oe in 626 CE was the son of Emperor Jomei and Empress Saimei. According to Traditional Order of Succession, he is the 38th monarch of Japan. His significant contributions to the nation were the Taika reforms, the Omi Code and the subduing of the Soga clan which held immense influence over the monarchy. He, conspiring with Nakatomi no Katamari (later given the title 'Fujiwara') assassinated Soga no Iruka and checked the re-insurgence of the Soga clan by dispersing their followers. This event, known as the Isshi Incident helped him gain the emperor's favor and was declared heir apparent. He ascended the throne in 661 CE after his mother and ruled as Emperor Tenji. Prince Naka no Oe contributed immensely to the codification of a series of reforms know as the Great Reforms or 'Taika Reforms' promulgated in 645 CE and as emperor Tenji, he enforced the oldest Japanese legal code known to modern historians, The Omi Code--a set of laws in 22 volumes in the last year of his reign. This Omi code formed the basis of all later legal codes and hold immense importance. He died in 672 CE, and Emperor Kobun succeeded him to the throne.

Empress Jito (645 - 703)

Jito was Emperor Tenchi's daughter and succeeded her husband Emperor Temmu (Tenchi's half-brother) as empress regnant becoming the third of the eight woman in to do so in Japanese history. She was born in 645 CE and ascended the throne in 686 CE after the death of her husband in order to secure succession for her son Prince Kasukabe. Throughout her reign, she ruled from the Fujiwara Palace or *Fujiwara no Miya* in the Yamato province. When Prince Kasukabe died, aged 27, Prince Karu-no-o was named Jito's successor who ultimately became Emperor Mommu.

Jito's reign is characterized by a stable government and politics. The Taika reforms and a group of deft statesmen added to its glory and the empire prospered. After reigning for 11 years, in 697 CE, Jito abdicated in favor of Karu-no-o who ascended the throne as Emperor Mommu. After her retirement, she took the title of 'retired emperor' or *Daijo-tenno* which was followed by her successors who took retirement from the throne. However she remained in politics and took part in court affairs till her death in 703 CE after which she was buried in *Ochi no Okanoe no Misasagi* a memorial Shinto shrine at Nara.

Kakinomoto no Hitomaro (? - 710)

Kakinomoto no Hitomaro was a famous Japanese scholar, aristocrat and poet of the late Asuka Period. His poems were included in large numbers in the first and second volume of the Man'yoshu and is considered to be one of the Thirty-six Poetry Immortals of Japan. His ancestry can be traced back to the 4th century aristocrats of Kasuga family, the descendants of Emperor Kosho who establish themselves as the officials of the Iwami province, a post that Hitomaro himself held at the age of fifty. He is particularly noted for long poems or *choka(s)* though he wrote a substantial number of shorter ones as well including the one found in the Ogura Hyakunin Isshu. Some of his famous poems include "The Bay of Tsunu", "I Love her like the leaves" and "Lament for Prince Takechi". Nineteen of his longer poems and about seventy-five shorter ones were selected to be included in the Man'yoshu and other imperial anthologies. He is often called the "Poet of Sounds" and his styles included rhyming(ouin), Pillow Words(*utamakura*) and other figures of speech like *makurakotoba, jokotoba* etc.

He stands high among all contemporary poets with his unique style of hymns and elegies. Several of his poems lament the death of friends and relatives and separation plays an important part among the themes that he wrote about. He served in the imperial court from about 680 CE till his death in 710 CE and was applauded for his poetic abilities. It is believed that empress Jito played an important motivational part in developing his genius. Ki no Tsurayuki, the compiler of the Kokin Waka-shu called him a genius among the divine immortal poets and a shrine dedicated to him is located at Akashi in the Hyogo Prefecture called Kakinomoto Jinja. An annual waka-contest is hosted by this shrine in his honor.

Yamabe no Akahito (700 - 736)

Akahito was considered a poetic genius and the best among the Nara poets. He lived approximately from 700 to 736 CE but his dates are debated. Thirteen of his *choka(s)* and thirty-seven *tanka(s)* found their way to the Man'yoshu. He is considered to be one of the *Kami(s)* of Gods of Waka poetry and is venerated to this day. He accompanied Emperor Shomu on his tour of the Eastern Provinces and most of his poems were composed during the journey i.e. Between 724 and 736 CE. I believe that this poem on Mount Fuji was also composed during this period thereby roughly establishing its time-period. However, more than this, very little is known about this great poet called *Waka Nisei* by the great poetry critic Ki no Tsurayuki in the Preface of the Kokin Waka-shu.

Sarumaru Dayu (?)

Very little can be known of Sarumaru Dayu if not nothing. He is also called Sarumaru no Taifu and is a poet of the early Heian period. He is included as one of the Thirty-Six Poetic Sages but nowhere else is he referred to. Even the ancient imperial anthologies are mute about his existence though the very poem attributed to him in the Ogura Hyakunin Isshu (5) is also found in the Kokin Waka-shu (4:215) Some believe that there never was any person called Sarumaru Dayu and it was Prince Yamashiro no Oe who used this name for poetry.

Otomo no Yakamochi (718 - 785)

Among towering figures in the Nara court, Otomo no Yakamochi tops the list. A multifaceted genius, he is considered one of the Thirty-Six Poetry Immortals of Japan and lived from, about 718 to 785 CE. He was one of the compilers of Japan's first poetic anthology, the Man'yoshu as well as a deft politician. His Otomo clan was engaged in military as well as bureaucratic activities in the Yamato court and Yakamochi himself rose to the post of *chunagon* or the highest bureaucratic official by virtue of his political acumen. In 740 CE, by orders of Emperor Shomu, he went to Kyushu to suppress the rebellion of Fujiwara no Hirotsugu and for the next ten years he remained the Governor of the Etchu Province. In 754 CE, military responsibilities were vested upon him and he became a commander. He conspired with Fujiwara no Yoshitsugu and plotted the assassination of Fujiwara no Nakamaro. Though he later abandoned the plan, on suspicion, he was transferred time and again from province to province. In 777 CE, he became Governor of the Ise Province that housed the Ise Grand Shrine dedicated to the Sun goddess Amaterasu. In 780, he was promoted to the post of *Sangi*. He died of drowning in the Matsu Province in 785 while working as the *shogun*, shortly after which Fujiwara no Tanetsugu was killed, sensing Yakamochi's involvement, he was denied a burial and posthumously excommunicated. His poetic works include several hundreds of *Choka* and *tanka* several of which are found in the Man'yoshu and other anthologies. He influenced the *Shika Waka-shu* as well and the famous Gunka song Umi Yukaba used one of his most famous and outstanding poem as lyrics, and was considered Japan's second anthem during wartime.

Abe no Nakamaro (ca. 698 - 770)

Nakamaro was the descendant of Prince Hikofutsoushi Makoto, the son of Emperor Kogen. As a young child, he was greatly admired for his academic abilities and mathematical acumen. He was an outstanding Japanese scholar, academician, politician and waka poet of the Nara Period. He was sent on a mission to T'ang China in 717 or 718 CE to learn Chinese methods of time calculation. Though others returned long ago, Nakamaro failed to come back to Japan. He passed the Chinese Civil-Service examination and in 725 CE he took up administrative posts and was promoted in Louyang in 728 ans 731. In 733 he took up the duty of managing Japanese diplomatic missions and in 734 tried to return to Japan but failed because of shipwrecks. He tried again and again to come back but bad luck dogged his steps. Finally in 755 he was tossed on the shores of Vietnam again because of a shipwreck. During the An Lashan Rebellion, he abandoned his hopes to return home and took-up several government posts in Vietnam including the Governor-General of Annam. He died in 770 CE, just when he was planning to return to Japan from Chang'an. The poem in the Hyakunin Isshu, that bears his name, is also found in the Kokin Waka-shu (9: 406).

Kisen Hoshi (Monk Kisen)

Very little is known of this solitary monk. He was probably a Buddhist priest who took to isolation out of weariness of the world and as he himself says dwelt on Mount Uji or Uji-yama. He is believed to have lived in the ending years of Nara, and the early years of the Heian period when Buddhism received a boost in Japan and its adherents increased rapidly. He is considered as one of the Six Poetic Sages of Japan by the critic Ki no Tsurayuki who writes about his work as follows: "The use of words is a delicate thing—from start to end it does not express the thing that actually is. That is to say, to speak of the autumn moon, he compares it to the clouds at dawn." He is said to be the author of a poetry collection "Waka-sakushiki" but this theory is debated. The only two poems that can be confidently attributed to Kisen are, the one that is included in the Ogura Hyakunin Isshu (8), as well as the Kokin Waka-shu (18: 983) and another one found in the Gyokuyo-shu (400).

Ono no Komachi (ca. 825 - 900)

Very little is known of this lady except the names of the various men who were romantically engaged with her. It is believed that she was the lady-of-the -bedchamber to Emperor Ninmyo but when he died, she started relationships with other men. She was (probably) born in the current Akita Prefecture to Yoshisad, the Lord of Dewa though her social status is yet uncertain. Her poetry is often said to be melancholic and full of anxiety, solitude and the typical styles that qualify the season Autumn. It is thus a surprise that the poem included in the Hyakunin Isshu was originally included in the Kokin Waka-shu (Number: 133) under the section dedicated to the season Spring. But as a woman of great beauty, Komachi leaves all other behind. In fact she is the only female poet referred to in the *kana* preface of the Kokin Waka-shu. That very preface describes her style to be "containing naivety in old style but also delicacy." There are a great number of legends surrounding Ono no Komachi; in fact some scholars think that there were several women referred to by that name because of their beauty. These legends developed in the eleventh century and were used extensively by the Noh play writers.

Semimaru(?)

Legend says Semimaru or Semimaro to be the son of Emperor Uda or the fourth son of Emperor Daigo. His blindness making him ineligible to the throne turned him into a hermit, poet and musician. But some claim that he was merely a sighted beggar. Anyhow, he built his hermitage at *Asuaka no Seki* (Osaka Barrier) or Meeting Hill which finds mention in his poem and was situated on a small hill near Lake Biwa not far away from the Imperial Capital, then at Kyoto. Some say that for some years Minamoto no Hiromasa tutored him in the Biwa (a musical instrument) though others claim that he was a maestro of the Biwa.

Probably this poem, also finds mention in the *Genji Monogatari* (The Tale of Genji, 1014 CE) where the coming and going at Ausaka Gate is mentioned. It is only natural for him to write of it, Ausaka Gate being an important checkpoint to the Capital. Mention of the Osaka-Barrier is also found in the 61st poem in a metaphoric sense. Semimaru's shrine at the Osaka Gate or the *Seki no Semimaru Jinja* is a popular tourist spot in Japan even today.

Sangi Takamura (802 - 853)

Sangi (Counselor) Takamura or Ono no Takamura was an early Heian period scholar, poet and counselor to the Emperor. There are a large number of strange tales about him including the one that says that at night he used to creep down to the underworld where he helped King Yama (the Devil) with his judgments. In 834 CE, he was appointed *kintoshi* but after a quarrel with the envoy Fujiwara no Tsunetsugu, he retired from his duties pretending to be ill. He then However, this great life of nobility was cut short when he refused to be a part of the 837 CE mission to T'ang China fearing the fearsome typhoons and the mayhem of the seas. This irked the reigning emperor Saga who banished him to the far off, north facing Oki Islands in the Japan Sea where Emperor Gotoba would be banished a few centuries later. The poem included here was composed while on his journey to the island and sent off to his home perhaps as a condolence message to his kinsfolk. He died presumably in the Oki islands in 853 CE. It is interesting to note that this same Takamura is the main character of a the famous story *"Takamura Monogatari"* of debated antiquity.

Sojo Henjo (816 - 890)

Sojo Henjo or monk Henjo was a Buddhist priest and a Waka poet. He is mentioned in the preface of the Kokin-Wakashu and he is listed among the Six Best Waka poets as well as the Thirty-Six Poetry Immortals of Japan. His birth-name was Yoshimine no Munesada and he was the eighth son of Yoshimine Yasuyo, one of the sons of Emperor Kammu. He began his career as a courtier and was given the status of a *kurodo*--a chamberlain in the court of Emperor Nimmyo. In 849 CE, he became the Head of the Kurodo but after Nimmyo's death(850) he became a monk out of grief. He was a priest of the Tendai school and in 877 CE, he founded the Gangyo-ji temple in the south-eastern part of the capital. In 869, he was appointed to manage the affairs at the Urin-In another temple, to the north of Kyoto. It 885, he was ranked *"Sojo"* and was hailed as Kazan Sojo. Thirty-five of his poems were included in the imperial anthologies including the Kokin-Wakashu whose editor Ki no Tsurayuki commented on his style saying: "he knows how to construct waka, but there is less real emotion. It is like when you see a picture of a woman and it moves your heart." He probably died in 890 CE and traditional chronicles ascertain the date of his death to be the 12th of February.

Emperor Yozei (869 - 949)

Emperor Yozei was the 57th Emperor of Japan as per the traditional order of succession and his rule spanned from 876 to 884 CE. His original name was Sadaakira Shinno and he was the oldest son of Emperor Seiwa whom he succeeded to the throne. Of the four noble clans of Japan, the Yozei Genji clan is said to have descended from Emperor Yozei. He was formally enthroned at the age of eight in the year 877 and became the all-encompassing ruler then on. In his formative years, he showed cruel and dangerous mentality and later came to be termed as mad. He used to feed live frogs to snakes or set monkeys and dogs to fight each other. He even chased off people who dared to speak up against him. Later, these cruel and despicable behaviors became more and more dangerous when they were extended to living human beings and the Kanpaku Fujiwara no Mototsune decided that the emperor was too undignified to rule and devised a plan to dethrone him. He set up a horse race and on the pretext of taking the emperor there, he redirected his carriage to "*Yo sei in*" palace in the town of *Ni Zio* and proclaimed the emperor's dethroning explaining to him his despicable actions (in 884) which had made him unfit to rule any longer. It is said that at this news the emperor cried sincerely and finally agreed to abdicate. He had nine Imperial sons after he abdicated and eventually Emperor Koko succeeded him to the throne.

Minamoto no Toru (822 - 895)

Minamoto no Toru was a Heian poet and scholar and was the grandson of Emperor Saga. He was thus a descendant of the Saga Genji clan and is attributed sometimes as the model for the role of Hikaru Genji in Lady Murasaki's masterful novel "*Genji Monogatari*" or the Tale of Genji. He was given the title of *Kawara no Sadaijin* meaning Riverbank

Minister of the Left and is assumed to have had prominent role in the Heian court though very little is known of him.

Emperor Koko (830 - 887)

Emperor Koko was the 58th emperor of Japan in the traditional order of succession and his coronation took place on the 23rd of March, 884 CE. His personal name was *"Tokiyatsu"* or *"Kamatsu-tei"* and he was the third son of Emperor Nimmyo. It is said that he solved the succession crisis simply be visiting the Tokiyatsu shrine where Kanpaku addressed him as the sovereign and he accepted the act by riding the imperial carriage to the Imperial residence. Emperor Koko was a stable politician unlike his predecessor and revived may an old court ritual. One if these was the imperial hawking excursion to *Serikawa*. It is said that he frequently traveled to Serikawa for hawking and enjoyed the exercise. He died at the age 57 in 887 CE and was buried at a memorial Shinto-shrine near Kyoto which is formally named as *"Kaguragaoka no Higashi no misasagi"*. The Imperial Household Agency designates it as the mausoleum of Emperor Koko.

Ariwara no Yukihira (818 - 893)

Yukihira was an eminent poet and prominent courtier in the Heian court and served under several posts which including that of the Chunagon (or councilor). At several points in his life he served as the Provincial Governors of Harima, Bizen, Shinano, Bitchu, Inaba etc. At the height of his career he was appointed as the Minister for Agriculture (*minbukyo*) and inspector of Mutsu and Dewa provinces. The poem included here was composed while or before leaving for Inaba province as its governor. He authored several poems and shared fame with his brother Narihira. It is said that he also established a school called Shogaku-in to educate the members of his clan.

Ariwara no Narihira (825 - 880)

Ariwara no Narihira along with his brother Yukihira shared fame of being one of the greatest poets of Japanese literature. He is included as one of the Six Best Waka poets as well as the Thirty-Six Poetry Immortals of Japan. He was the fifth son of Prince Abo, a son of Emperor Heizei and his mother was Princess Ito a daughter of Emperor Kammu. In spite of descending from Emperors on both maternal and paternal sides, he had very little prestige at court. However, he and his brothers were relegated to civilian live and was given a new clan-name--Ariwara. He is said to have had a secret love affair with the empress Fujiwara no Takaiko (mentioned in poem 17) and that is sighted as the main reason why he was not given any prominent position in the court particularly under the reign of Emperor Montoku. He is another person considered to have influenced the character of Genji in Murasaki's novel (particularly in the aspect of forbidden love). His love affairs were also the subject of 'The Tales of Ise' and other stories. For a long period of time he was considered the finest poet of Japanese literature and so has been mentioned in the preface of the Kokin-Wakashu by Ki no Tsurayuki. He is also mentioned in Sei Shonagon's Pillow Book as one of her favourite poets.

All together, thirty of his waka poems have been included in the Imperial anthology--*Kokin Wakashu* and Narihira continues to be one of the most prominent poets of the Heian period if not a prominent character at all.

Fujiwara no Toshiyori (? - 901 or 907)

Very less is knows of the life of Fujiwara no Toshiyori. He was a middle Heian courtier, nobleman and an accomplished Waka poet. He is designated as one of the Thirty-Six Poetry Immortals of Japan and several of his poems have been included in the *Kokin Wakashu*, the *Gosen Wakashu* and the *Ogura Hyakunin Isshu*. He had his own collection of poems called the *Toshiyuki-shu* and died sometime in the very early tenth century.

Lady Ise (875 - 938)

Lady Ise was among the first group of female poets of the Hyakunin Isshu. She was born to Fujiwara no Tsugukage, of the Ise Province whereby, she gets her sobriquet, and became a lover of Prince Atsuyoshi. She was a concubine of Emperor Uda and bore him a son—Prince Yuki-Akari. She wrote in a characteristic style of her times and was emblematic of that changing style. Twenty-two of her poems were included in the *Kokin-Wakashu* and one in the Ogura Hyakunin Isshu. She also had a private collection of poems called the *Ise-shu* and her poems are both genius and prominent in the Imperial anthologies.

Prince Mototoshi (890 - 943)

Prince Mototoshi was the eldest son of Emperor Yozei but unlike his mad father, he was a stable and intelligent nobleman. He is also revered as a great lover. Twenty of his poems were included in the Imperial anthology, the *Gosen-Wakashu* and one in the Hyakunin Isshu. He married one of the daughters of Emperor Daigo and Emperor Uda and is said to have a personal collection of poems entitles the *Mototoshi-Shinno-shu*.

Dhamma-Master Sosei (ca. 844 - 910)

Sosei Hoshi was the son of Dhamma-Master Henjo and took tonsure sometime after his father. He was a prolific poet prominently mentioned in the *Kokin-Wakashu* and was also included as one of the Thirty-Six Poetry Immortals of Japan. He was a popular poet of his time when the Buddhist church was not as institutionalized as it would become later. So he used to enjoy contact with the Imperial Court and took part in poetry competitions.

Fun'ya no Yasuhide (? - ca. 855)

Fun'ya no Yasuhide was a prolific poet of Japanese literature though very little is known of him. He lived in the early Heian period and was included in the *Rokkasen* and the Thirty Six Poetry Immortals of Japan. It is believed that he attained the Upper Sixth Rank and in *Tsurayuki*'s preface to the Kokinshu, he is mentioned, and of his style, Tsurayuki writes, "Yasuhide, used words skillfully, but his words do not match the content. His poetry is like a merchant dressed up in elegant clothes." Five of his poems are included in the Kokin Waka-shu and one in the Goshui-Waka-shu. He is said to have been in a relationship with Ono no Komachi but this view is debatable. His son was also a popular poet--Fun'ya no Asayasu.

Oe no Chisato (?)

Oe no Chisato's exact dates are unknown but he is believed to have lived sometime between the late ninth and the early tenth century. He was not only a a waka poet but also a Confucian scholar. Prominent mention of him is found between the years 889 and 923 CE. He was one of the Thirty Six Poetry Immortals of Japan and was the nephew of Ariwara no Narihira and Yukihira. Ten of his poems were included in the Kokin Waka-shu and another fifteen in later anthologies. He was a son of Oe no Otondo however, very little information on him is available.

Sugawara no Michizane (845 - 903)

Michizane is probably one of the most respected poets of the Ogura Hyakunin Isshu. Today, he is revered as the God of Learning or Tenman-Tenjin. He was also known as Kan Shojo or Kanke and was a Heian poet, scholar and politician of great repute. He challenged the powerful Fujiwara family and was sent into exile for that crime. His grandfather first entered into scholarly education and passed on this tradition onto his son Koreyoshi and grandson Michizane. They actively worked for the adoption of Chinese tradition and literature and helped in editing the Imperial anthologies in Chinese. They also served as professors in the Chinese-oriented Court University (*Daigaku-ryo*) and helped in the percolation of Confucian ethics into Heian Japan.

He began his studies of the Chinese classics and composed his first poem at the age of eleven. in 862 CE, he entered the university and in 870, he passed the Civil Service Examination and entered into the court bureaucracy. In 877, he was appointed a professor of Chinese Literature after holding several minor posts. During that period, he greeted two embassies from China. He quickly rose to great power under Emperor Uda who wanted to rule without Fujiwara interference. In 886, he was appointed a governor of Sanuki Province for an extended period of time which led to a long period of lamentation. In 901, after Emperor Daigo came to the throne and the Fujiwaras now securing an upper hand falsely accused him of plotting against the throne and he was exiled to Kyushu Province where he died in 903 CE. Among his literary achievements, he is famed to have helped in the writing of the *Nihon Sandai Jitsuroku* or "The True History of the Three Reigns of Japan." and the compilation of Japan's Six Official Histories (the *Rikkokushi*). Although he found disgrace towards the end of his life, today, he is revered as a God of Learning. Shrines dedicated to him were established in Kyoto named *Kitano Tenman-gu* and Tokyo called *Yushima Tenman-gu*.

Fujiwara no Sadakata (873 - 932)

Fujiwara no Sadakata is also known as *Sanjo Udaijin*. He was a Japanese poet and scholar or some reputation.

He was the son of Fujiwara no Takafuji and his cousin and son-in-law was the poet Fujiwara no Kanesuke. His son was Fujiwara no Asatada--also a poet of great reputation. However, in spite of his fame, very less is known of him. He seems to have attained high post in court.

Fujiwara no Tadahira (880 - 949)

Tadahira was a Heian Japanese statesman, scholar and poet. He is credited for composing the *Engishiki* (a collection of Japanese traditions and rituals). He was a *kuge* (Japanese bureaucrat) and was responsible for the development of the Japanese legal code called *"Sandai Kyaku-shiki"*. Tadahira served as regent under Emperor Suzaku (r. 930 - 46) and from 914 to 941 CE, he served at various positions from the *udaijin* to the *daijo-daijin* and ultimately *Kampaku* (in 941). He was the son of Fujiwara no Mototsune and was the head of the Hokke branch of the Fujiwara clan since 909 CE. He married the daughter of Emperor Koko and had several children including Fujiwara no Saneyori--another poet included in the Hyakunin Isshu.

Fujiwara no Kanesuke (877 - 933)

Kanesuke Fujiwara was a middle Heian scholar, poet and nobleman. He is included as one of the Thirty-Six Poetry Immortals of Japan and his poems are a part of the Imperial anthologies such as the Kokin Waka-shu and Gosen Waka-shu. He also had a personal collection of poems called the *Kanesuke-shu* and is believed to be a famous poet of his time.

He is also said to be the great-grandfather of Lady Murasaki, authoress of the first novel of the world--The Tale of Genji.

Fujiwara no Muneyuki (? - 983)

Muneyuki is mentioned as one of the Thirty-Six Poetry Immortals of Japan but only vague details are available on his life. He is believed to be a nobleman. His personal collection of poetry is called the *Muneyuki-shu.*

Oshikochi no Mitsune (859 - 925)

Oshikochi no Mitsune was another member of the Thirty-Six Poetry Immortals of Japan and was sent to the provinces of Kai, Izumi and Awaji as the governor. Upon his return to the capital, he was asked to participate in the compilation of the *Kokin Waka-shu* and with this his fame was elevated to an immense height. He was famous for the pictures that accompanied his poetry for folding screens. With his large number of poems, he is often regarded as a parallel or worthy competitor of Ki no Tsurayuki and many of these poems were included in the various imperial anthologies including the *Kokin Waka-shu.*

Mibu no Tadamine (898 - 920)

Mibu no Tadamine apparently rose to fame from nowhere in an early Heian poetry competition or *utawase.* That competition is famous as the "Poetry Match at Prince Koresada's Residence" held sometime around 893 CE. After that he became very involved in poetic activities in and around the capital and also took part in the compilation of the *Kokin Waka-shu*. He is said to have a poetry collection of his own entitled *Tadamine-shu*. He is also famous for his work 'Ten Styles of Tadamine' or *Tadamine-Juttei* but other facts of his life remain greatly obscure.

Sakanoue no Korenori (?)

Korenori was a Heian period Waka poet. His exact dates are unknown but he is believed to be a fourth-generation descendant of Sakanoue no Tamuramaro. He is said to be a champion *kemari* player and legends of his skills survive to this date. He is included as one of the Thirty-Six Poetry Immortals of Japan and forty-one of his poems found their way to the imperial anthologies. His political life was also illustrious coming in the spotlight probably because of his poetic and athletic skills, he served as the governors of Kaga Province.

Harumichi no Tsuraki (? - 920)

Very little is known of Tsuraki except that he died in the year 920 CE just a he was about to take charge as the Governor of Iki Province. He is believed to have graduated from the Imperial University in 910 CE. Altogether five of his poems have found their ways to the imperial anthologies--the *Kokin Wakashu* and the *Gosen Wakashu*. Compared to the other poets of the Hyakunin Isshu, his fame seems almost negligible and it is a marvel that his poem was at all included in this special collection.

Ki no Tomonori (ca. 850 - 904)

Tomonori like several other Heian scholar-poets was involved in the compilation of the *Kokin Waka-shu* however, was not lucky enough to see its completion. He died before the work was complete and Ki no Tsurayuki included a eulogy to him in that very anthology. He has a number of poems attributed to him in the anthologies commissioned by the emperor including the *Kokin Waka-shu* and a few later ones and is also known to have a personal collection of poems named the *Tomonori-shu*. He was also included as a member of the Thirty-Six Poetry Immortals by Kinto.

Fujiwara no Okikaze (?)

Details about Okikaze's life are extremely vague. He is believed to be a middle Heian *Waka* poet. He is believed to be an illustrious poet and has several of his poems included in the *Kokin Waka-shu* as well as the other imperial anthologies. He also appears to have a personal collection of poems called *Okikaze-shu*.

Ki no Tsurayuki (872 - 945)

Ki no Tsurayuki was a Heian period poet, author and courtier of some reputation. In 890 CE, he started his career as a waka poet and rose to some fame. Receiving orders from Emperor Daigo, he started compilation of the *Kokin Waka-shu* After holding a few offices in Kyoto he was appointed as the Governor of the Tosa Province (930 - 935) where probably he wrote the Tosa Diary (*Tosa Nikki*). After that probably he became the governor of Sue province

He was well known for his poetic compositions and was counted as one of the Thirty Six Poetry Immortals of Japan by Kinto. He composed one of the prefaces of the *Kokin Waka-shu* and probably wrote the first criticism of waka poetry in his preface. He is even referred to as a waka-master in Murasaki's novel 'The Tale of Genji'.

Kiyohara no Fukayabu (?)

Fukayabu was a relatively well-known poet of his time. He was the grandfather of Kiyohara no Motosuke and the great-grandfather of Sei Shonagon. He was a poet of the middle Heian period and contributed 17 poems to the *Kokin Waka-shu*.

Fun'ya no Asayasu (late 9th - early 10th century)

Fun'ya no Asayasu was the son of Fun'ya no Yasuhide and seems to have had some reputation as a waka poet. He lived during the height of the Heian period but little is known about him in general. The poem included in this anthology seems to have been composed in the year 900 at the request of Emperor Daigo. Yet, Asayasu's fame is much less compared to some of the other poets of the same period gaining favour with the sovereign.

Lady Ukon (?)

Lady Ukon or *"Ukon Shikibu"* takes her sobriquet after her father's post in the Court which was of Lesser Captain of the Right Bodyguards (*ukon-e no shosho*). She had an active career as a poet for about thirty years. In 933, she composed a poem celebrating the coming off age of Princess Koshi and she also took part in poetry competitions at the court in 960, 962, and 966 CE. She is said to have a large number of romantic affairs with various men and she exchanged letters with Prince Motoyoshi, Fujiwara no Atsutada, Fujiwara no Morosuke, Fujiwara no Morouji, Fujiwara no Asatada and Minamoto no Shitago. Her fame was elevated by the inclusion of her name in the list of the Thirty-Six Female Poetry Immortals of Japan. She is believed to have been deserted by her husband in her married life. Her poetic works were included in the *Gosen Waka-shu* compiled later on.

Minamoto no Hitoshi (880 - 951)

Minamoto no Hitoshi is referred to by the title *"Sangi"* which alludes to his high rank in the court and Professor Mostow believes that he held many important as well as minor posts in the political sphere but his career as a poet remains largely obscure. He has four poems included in the Imperial anthologies that too in the *Gosen Waka-shu*. The poem included here, seems to have been sent to a woman or composed in response to some other poem.

Taira no Kanemori (? - 990)

Taira no Kanemori is regarded as the representative poet of the *Gosenshu* period. The Gosenshu was the second imperial anthology ordered in 950 CE. Three of his poems were included in the Gosen-shu though under the hood of anonymity. Altogether, he contributed eighty-six poems in the various imperial anthologies of which thirty-eight were included in the *Shuishu* alone. He is revered as a poetry immortal of Japan of the later periods. The poem included in the Ogura Hyakunin Isshu is believed to have been written at a poetry competition held as the Court in 960 CE.

Mibu no Tadami (ca. 945 - 980)

Mibu no Tadami was a middle Heian Waka poet and a scholar. He is regarded as a master of poetic compositions and is said to have had great pride presenting himself thus. In the competition held in 960 CE, Tadami was defeated and is said to have been severely criticised and depressed after that incident. Some sources say that he took his life out of grief but some other sources suggest that he was alive well after 960 CE. His poems are included in several poetry collections and he is regarded as one of the Thirty-Six Poetry Immortals. He also has a personal collection of poems called *"Tadami-shu"*

Kiyohara no Motosuke (908 - 990)

Motosuke was, as all the others, a middle Heian nobleman and waka poet. He is credited for assisting in the compilation of the *Gosen Waka-shu* as a part of the Five Men of the Pear Chamber. His poems are included in several imperial anthologies including the *Shui Waka-shu*. In his political life, he became the Governor of Higo and Kawachi provinces and gained favour with the Imperial sovereign. It must also be worthwhile to mention that this illustrious figure was the father of the famous Sei Shonagon and kept a personal collection of poems called "*Motosuke-shu*".

Fujiwara no Atsutada (906 - 943)

Atsutada was the third son of the powerful minister Tokihira and a middle Heian poet. His genius in poetic compositions is frequently praised in the Tales of Yamato and a lot of his poems in correspondence with court ladies survive. He is well represented in the *Gosen Waka-shu* and is also considered one of the Thirty Six Poetry Immortals of Japan. Owing to his political position, he is also called *Hoin-Chunagon or Gon-Chunagon* roughly signifying "Chancellor."

Fujiwara no Asatada (910 - 966)

Chunagon Asatada was a middle Heian nobleman and waka poet designated as one of the Thirty-Six Poetry Immortals of Japan. He won favour with the Imperial Sovereign and rose to prominent position in the poetry-circle. His poems are included in the Imperial anthologies such as the *Gosen Waka-shu* etc. and a personal collection of poems called *Asatada-shu* exists.

Fujiwara no Koremasa (924 - 972)

Koremasa also mentioned as Fujiwara no Koretada, was Heian nobleman and political figure of some importance. He served as regent (970) under the Emperor En'yu. Throughout his political career, he served under various posts including that of the *Udaijin, Sessho,* and *Daijo-daijin.* If his political life was glamorous, so was his poetic life. He was frequently involved in compilations and his poetry finds prominent mention in the *Gosen Waka-shu* and later imperial anthologies. His poems were published in the 'Collected Poems of the First Ward Regent" or "*Ichijo Sessho Gyoshu*" and one of them also finds its way to the Ogura Hyakunin Isshu whereby we encounter Koremasa lamenting his plight.

Sone no Yoshitada (?)

Yoshitada served as the Secretary of the Tango province and hence was also referred to as "Sotango". Though his dates are unknown, it is believed that he flourished in the later part of the tenth century. Numerous stories mention him as an eccentric person but later, probably after his death, he came to be revered as a truly innovative poet. About ninety of his poems are included in the imperial anthologies and he was included as one of the Thirty-Six Poetry Immortals of Japan.

Priest Egyo (?)

Dhamma-master Egyo was a Japanese Buddhist monk and poet actively working during the last part of the tenth century. Professor Mostow explains that he was closely associated with the other contemporary poets of repute and they all frequently met at the *Kawara Mansion* on the banks of the Kamo river. Among his associates Yoshinobu and Motosuke appear as stalwarts. The poem included here, seems to have been composed at such a meeting under a topic: "Dilapidated House." Egyo beautifully intertwines the topic of the competition with his own Buddhist philosophies and tenets of effervescence of life.

Minamoto no Shigeyuki (? - 1001)

Shigeyuki was a reputed Heian waka poet and a nobleman well associated with Kanemori (poem 40) and Sanekata (poem 51). He is the last of the Thirty-Six Poetry Immortals of Japan and is believed to have died in the first years of the eleventh century. He kept a personal collection of poems named *Shigeyuki-shu*.

Onakatomi no Yoshinobu (921 - 991)

Yoshinobu was a Heian poet and nobleman or great repute. He was the grandfather of the later Japanese poetess Ise no Taiyu and is designated as a member of the Thirty-Six Poetry Immortals of Japan. He was also a member of the Five Men of the Pear Chamber and assisted the compilation of the *Gosen Waka-shu* as well as the *kundoku*. Yoshinobu's poems are found in great numbers in the *Shui Waka-shu* and a personal collection of poems called the *Yoshinobu-shu* exists till date.

Fujiwara no Yoshitaka (954 - 975)

Almost nothing in known about Yoshitaka or Yoshitake except some very basic facts that tell almost nothing in relation to the poem included in the anthology. He was the third son of Koremasa and father of the calligrapher Yukinari. He is considered as one of the Late Classical Thirty-Six Poetry Immortals of Japan. It is known that Yoshitaka lost his life early at the age of twenty one and that he probably died of small-pox. Altogether twelve of his poems were included in the *GoShui-shu* and later imperial anthologies. A personal collection of poems also exists in his name.

Fujiwara no Sanekata (ca. 954 - 994)

Sanekata was the great-grandson of Tadahira and was highly regarded as a great Heian scholar and poet. He is one of the Late Classical Thirty-Six Poetry Immortals of Japan and has about sixty-seven of his poems included in the various imperial anthologies including the *Shuishu*. The poem by his included in the Ogura Hyakunin Isshu is said to have been sent to a woman. He was particularly known for his poems on love.

Fujiwara no Michinobu (972 - 994)

Fujiwara no Michinobu was the adopted son of Fujiwara no Kane'ie, the husband of the poetess of the following poem. It seems that the philandering reputation of Michinobu was passed down even to his adopted son and he had a couple of affairs as well. Anyhow, Michinobu died at the tender age of twenty-three but left a legacy of poems most of which belong to the category of *kinuginu no uta* or "morning after poems." He left forty-eight poems in the imperial anthologies and also had a personal poetry collection.

Michitsuna no Haha (ca. 937 - 995)

The actual name of the poet of the 53rd poem of the Ogura Hyakunin Isshu is not known. He is simply mentioned as "Michitsuna no Haha" which literally means "Mother of Michitsuna". She is and illustrious person on Japanese literature particularly for her autobiographical diary--the "*Kagero Nikki*" or "Gossamer Years". She was a minor wife of Fujiwara no Kane'ie and is said to have been dissatisfied at the state of the marriage. Legend says that she was one of the three most beautiful women of her time and that she was also one of the most accomplished female poets. She is included as one of the Late Classical Thirty-Six Poetry Immortals of Japan and contributed thirty-six poems to the various imperial anthologies including the *Shuishu*.

Ko no Naishi (? - 996)

Lady Ko also known as "Takako" or Kishi was the wife of Fujiwara no Michitaka and the mother of Empress Teishi. She is recognized simply by the name *"Gioshanshi no Haha"* or Mother of the Supernumerary Grand Minister owing to the immense power wielded by her son Fujiwara no Korechika. Takako was from an elite family and is said to have possessed some talent in Chinese poetry which drove her to win many poetry competitions. She composed the poem included here shortly after her marriage to Michitaka out of sheer excitement. But unfortunately that joy proved shortlived and with Michitaka's early death, Takako also took tonsure and lived her life as a Buddhist in seclusion.

Fujiwara no Kinto (966 - 1041)

Fujiwara no Kinto is yet another important figure in the cultural history of Japan and stands on equal footing with people like Hitomaro, Narihira, Tsurayuki and probably even, Lady Murasaki. He was also a great calligrapher and was frequently mentioned by Sei Shonagon and Lady Murasaki themselves in their respective works. He was the son of the regent Fujiwara no Yoritada and the father of the illustrious Fujiwara no Sadayori. Throughout his life, Kinto published many works and was instrumental to the compilation of the *Shui Waka-shu* compiled by order of Emperor Kazan between 996 and 999 CE. He also established the "Thirty Six Poetry Immortals of Japan" and set apart the thirty-six poets he considered to be of outstanding genius. His poems frequently feature in the *Shui Waka-shu* and the

Wakan Reoishu of which the former contains fifteen of his poems.

Lady Izumi (ca. 976 - ?)

Izumi Shikibu or Lady Izumi was one of the prosperous female poets in service under Empress Joto Mon'in. In fact, the era in which Lady Izumi lived, produced the most illustrious female authors and poets Japan has ever produced including Ekazome Emon, Sei Shonagon and the legendary Lady Murasaki. Unfortunately, Lady Izumi's original name remains unknown to this date. However, there are certain assumptions which lack solid grounding as to what it might have been. Like other female authors of her time, she used the province which her husband was the governor of, as her sobriquet. At the age of 20, she married Tachibana no Michisada, the governor of Izumi province. In spite of being married, Izumi Shikibu maintained a large number of love affairs one of which, with Prince Tamekata, became a major scandal and Michisada divorced her. She even got disinherited by her father. Later she also indulged in relationships with Price Atsumichi whereby after a lot of complications, she moved into Atsumichi's residence. However though she became famous, she never probably got a happy married life. Atsumichi died a few years after this affair and Izumi entered the court of Fujiwara no Shoshi who was the daughter of Michinaga and a consort of Emperor Ichijo. Yet, she went on to be one of the iconic poets of Heian times and one of the Thirty-Six Poetry Immortals of Japan. Among her iconic works is her autobiographical diary *Izumi Shikibu-nikki* and a great number of poems.

Her scandalous love affairs are hinted in the stories like *Eiga-Monogatari* and *Rekishi-Monogatari*. In her career, Lady Izumi won the title of the "Floating Lady" or *ukareme* from Michinaga because of the great passion and love in her life. Her poetry style was rather sentimental and was directly in opposition to the style of a close friend--Ekazome Emon. She also entered into severe competition with Lady Murasaki who also served in the same court. Lady Izumi's poems are often seen to lament the death or wilting of life. She is said to have married Fujiwara no Yasumasa later and accompanied him to the Tango Province when he became the governor. The year of her death is unknown but she is believed to have had a long life. The last correspondence from her is dated 1033 CE.

Murasaki Shikibu (ca. 973 - 1014 or 1031)

Among all the hundred poets of the Ogura Hyakunin Isshu, no one left a more lasting mark on world literature than Lady Murasaki or Murasaki Shikibu. Murasaki Shikibu is famous for being the first novelist of the world and her novel *Genji Monogatari* or the Tale of Genji is a masterpiece of world literature. However, her fame of being a novelist often eclipses Murasaki's fame as a poet. Ever since childhood Murasaki had been considered a prodigy and was among the very few women to receive education similar to men. She was given lessons in Chinese classics which was otherwise restricted to men of noble birth only. Even by lineage, she was the granddaughter of Fujiwara no Kanesuki--a famous poet and scholar and thus received ample support from her family to develop her genius.

Widowed early after a shorty marriage to an officer of the Imperial Guard--Fujiwara no Nobutaka (998 CE), she was called to the court by the imperial consort Akiko and given the post of a "Maid of Honour" to Empress Shoshi in 1005 CE. It is not exactly known since when she started using the sobriquet "Murasaki" probably taken from the famous character Murasaki in her novel. She composed the "Tale of Genji" at the imperial court and soon it began to circle around the capital and Murasaki's reputation received a major boost. However, according to Louis Perez, since childhood, Murasaki was "pretentious, awkward, difficult to approach, prickly, too fond of her tales, haughty, prone to versifying, disdainful, cantankerous and scornful." Nobutaka and Murasaki's daughter was the famous poet Daini no Sanmi.

Apart from her novel, Lady Murasaki is also known for her Diary which contains a large number of her poems. It is said that after her husband's death, she retreated to *Ishiyama-dera* near Lake Biwa and that she was inspired to write the Tale of Genji staring at the August moon over the lake. In her diary, Lady Murasaki narrates long descriptive passages as well as poems. She started writing her diary when she entered into service of Empress Shoshi; it covers the period from 1008 to 1010.

Apart from the Diary, she also wrote the *Poetic Memoirs*--a set of 128 poems arranged in biographical order. It is said that it was Fujiwara no Teika who published Lady Murasaki's poems in 1206 CE.

Daini no Sanmi (?)

Daini no Sanmi was a *waka* poet of the mid-Heian period. She was the daughter of the illustrious Murasaki Shikibu and Fujiwara no Nobutaka. She was given the name *Kenshi* and was married to Takashina no Nariakina. Altogether thirty-eight of her poems were included in the *Gosen Wakashu* and other imperial anthologies. A personal collection of poems called *Daini-no-Sanmi-shu* also exists.

Ekazome Emon (956 - 1041)

Ekazome Emon was a waka poet and an early historian living in the mid-Heian period. She is a member of the Thirty-Six Elder Poetic Sages as well as the Thirty-Six Female Poetic Sages and a daughter of Ekazome Tokimochi. She was married to Oe no Masahira--a famous literary scholar. However, in 1012, Masahira drowned and after his death, Emon is said to have lost interest in worldly matters. She served Empress Shoshi as well as her mother Genrinshi and was present at the Imperial court at the same time as Izumi Shikibu. She was heavily praised by Murasaki Shikibu and was also a contemporary of Sei Shonagon. She took part in the poetry competitions held in 1035 and 1041. He poetry collection was published as the *Ekazome-Emon-shu* and she was also the chief author of the *Eiga Monogatari* which is an epic that records the history of the Fujiwara clan and serves as a follow up to the Rikkokushi. Her poems were also included in the anthologies like *Shika Wakashu* and *Shui Wakashu*.

Ko-shikibu no Naishi (? - 1025)

Naishi was a *waka* poet who wrote in the eleventh century and is said to have died early, still in her twenties. She was the daughter of Izumi Shikibu and Tachibana no Michisada--the governor of Mutsu province. Around 1009 CE, she joined her mother and served under Empress Shoshi. She is said to have been the target of many suitors but eventually married Fujiwara no Kiminari. She had a son; but died soon thereafter.

Ise no Taifu (?)

Ise no Taifu was a *waka* poet working in the 11th century. She was the granddaughter of a great waka poet Onakatomi no Yoshinobu. She is included as one of the later Thirty-Six Poetry Immortals of Japan.

Sei Shonagon (ca. 966 - 1020)

Sei Shonagon was an illustrious Japanese author and court-lady who served Empress Teishi sometime around 1000 CE. Her actual name is not known, as per court customs of the day, she was known by her sobriquet Sei Shonagon. 'Sei' is the classical Japanese reading of the family name of her father *Kiyohara* ['kiyo'= "sei"]. Shonagon was the post that her father held at the court (that of, lesser councilor of state). There is a possibility that her given name was Kiyohara no Nagiko but the theory is debated. Details of her life are scarcely known and what is known mostly is from her own writings. She married a government official Tachibana no Norimitsu at 16 and gave birth to a son. In 993, at the age of 27, she entered into the service of Empress Teishi consort to Emperor Ichijo. She is famous for writing her *Pillow Book* or 'Makura no Soshi' where she writes of the daily-life at the court and the gossips, poetry, observations etc. Circulating among the court-circles. Her focus in thee Pillow Book was to pass on the observations of the daily court-life to the future world she speaks about the Empress Teishi and her sad demise after childbirth. The Pillow Book is a great source of information on the etiquette and mannerisms of her times. The Pillow Book only records events upto the year 1010 and no information about her is found after 1017 CE. It is said that she died as a Buddhist monk in poverty though another theory says that she lived on to marry Fujiwara no Muneyo--the governor of Setsu province and that she had a daughter named Myobu. Though she is mainly remembered as an author, she is also a poet of no less importance.

Fujiwara no Michimasa (992 - 1054)

Michimasa was the nephew of Empress Teishi and a mid-Heian period *waka* poet and court noble. He was the son of Fujiwara no Korechika and a granddaughter of Fujiwara no Michitaka. At the early age of fourteen, Michimasa was conferred the Junior Lower Fifth rank. He held several other offices during his career at the court including that of the servant of the future emperor Ichijo, Lieutenant of the Guards of the Left (1015) and other. In September of 1016 he was escorting the Imperial princess Masako to the Ise Shrine to become the High-Priestess. Their affair was disclosed and the sovereign and the reiterd Emperor Sanjo heavily punished him for his deed. In 1024 Emperor Kazan's daughter Jotomo-In was murdered and the murderer confessed that he had murdered under Michimasa's orders. Thus Michimasa was demoted from his posts. In July, 1054, he took tonsure out of grief and died very soon. Five of his poems were included in the *Goshui Wakashu* and two in the *Shika Wakashu*.

Fujiwara no Sadayori (995 - 1045)

Fujiwara no Sadayori was the son of the great Fujiwara no Kinto. He was entrusted with the post of "Supernumerary Middle-Councilor". On his mother's side we descended from Emperor Murakami. It is said that he was also given certain military responsibilities. The 60th poem in this anthology by Ko-shikibu is said to have been dedicated to him. He was a *waka* poet and calligrapher of great renown and was included as one of the Late Classical Thirty-Six Poetic Geniuses. Forty-five of his poems were included in the imperial anthologies and a personal poetry collection of him also exists.

Lady Sagami (ca. 1000 - ?)

Lady Sagami was the daughter of Minamoto no Yorimitsu and appears in many tales and Noh plays as a famous female character of the day. She was married to Oe no Kin'yori who was the governor of Sagami province (modern Kanagawa) whereby she derives her sobriquet. She was a famous *waka* poet and participated in many poetry competitions. She had one-hundred and nine of her poems included in the imperial anthologies and also a personal collection of poems. She is one of the Late Classical Thirty-Six Poetic Geniuses.

Archbishop Gyoson (1055 - 1135)

Gyoson was the son of Minamoto no Motohira and taking tonsure, he joined the Onjoji (or Miidera) Temple in Otsu. He was a practitioner of the *Shugendo* rites of the *yamabushi* mountain ascetics. In 1123 CE, he became the Archbishop of Enryakuji--the most important temple of the Tendai sect. He was also the Chief Almoner to Emperor Shirakawa and Emperor Toba. He contributed forty-eight poems to the Imperial anthologies and also left a personal poetry collection.

Lady Suo (?)

Lady Suo or Nakako was the daughter of Taira no Munenaka, the governor of Suo province. She served as a handmaiden to four emperors beginning with Emperor Go-Reizei to Emperor Horikawa. She took into religion in 1108 and died soon after that. Altogether, thirty-five of her poems are included in the imperial anthologies and she also left a personal collection. She derives her sobriquet from the name of the province that her father governed.

Emperor Sanjo (976 - 1017)

Emperor Sanjo was the son of Emperor Reizei and was the sixty-seventh emperor of Japan reigning from 1011 to 1016 CE. He became crown-prince in 986 CE but after a short reign was forced to retire due to his bad health and other political complications. Eight of his poems found palace in the imperial anthologies.

Priest Noin (988 - 1051)

Priest Noin's original name was Tachibana no Nagayasu. He came to be called Noin after taking tonsure. He was a Japanese *waka* poet and monk of the late Heian period and authored of the *Gengen-shu* and Noin's *Utakamuka*. He was selected as one of the Thirty-Six Medieval Poetry Immortals.

Priest Ryosen (?)

Ryosen Hoshi or Dhamma-Master Ryosen was a Buddhist priest and *waka* poet of the late Heian period. Though his dates are uncertain, he is seen to be active during the reigns of Emperor Go-Suzaku (1036 - 1045) and Go-Reizei (1045 - 1068). He participated in several poetry competitions and contributed thirty-one poems to the imperial anthologies particularly the *Go-Shuishu*.

Minamoto no Tsunenobu (1016 - 1097)

Major Councilor Tsunenobu (or *Dainagon Tsunenobu*) was a famous poet and progenitor of a long line of poets.

He was the grandfather of Shun'e (poem 85) and the father of Toshiyori (poem 74). He makes his poetic debut at a competition known as the "Poetry Contest on Famous Place Names at the Residence of Princess Yushi" (*Yushi naishinno-ke Meisho Utaawase.*) He is said to be a rival of Fujiwara no Mochitoshi and have compiled a counter-collection of Mochitoshi's *Go-Shui-shu.* He kept a personal collection of his poetry and contributed eighty-six poems to the *GoShuishu* and other imperial anthologies.

Lady Kii (?)

Yushi Naishinno-ke no Kii was the daughter of Taira no Tsunekata and Lady KoBen who also served under Imperial princess Yushi. She was an acclaimed poet and took part in several competitions. Her personal collection of poetry is known as *Ichi-no-Miya no Kii-shu* drawing from another of her sobriquets. Altogether she contributed thirty-one poems to the various imperial anthologies including the *GoShuishu.*

Oe no Masafusa (1041 - 1111)

Masafusa was particularly very close to Emperor Horikawa. He participated in several poetry competitions including the Horikawa Hyaku-shu. He was a well versed poet in Japanese as well as Chinese ans was the source of many books including the *Godan-Sho,* a collection of anecdotes and a collection of his poetry the *Go no Sochi Shu.* He contributed 119 poems to the *GoShuishu* and other imperial anthologies.

Minamoto no Toshiyori (1055 - 1129)

Toshiyori, also known as Shunrai was a rather innovative Japanese poet and is credited for having compiled the *Gosen-shu*. He was the son of Tsunenobu and held the second rank in the court. He gained favour with Emperor Go-Sanjo and also to a certain degree with Emperor Shirakawa. This alliance between the Minamoto family (rivals of the dominating Fujiwaras) and the Emperor is seen as a political alliance by many scholars. By allying against the Fujiwaras, the emperor gave the Minamoto's a chance to strike back at the Fujiwara (or their branch family--the Rokujo.) After writing a severe criticism of the Goshui-Wakashu named the *Nan-Goshui*, he somehow convinced Emperor Shirakawa to permit him to compile the next imperial anthology--the *Kin'yo Waka-shu*. After its publication however, a lot of courtiers began to criticize his work and his fame deteriorated. The *Gosen Waka-shu* became the subject of severe criticism and mockery. Towards the end of his life, Toshiyori composed a poetic treaties known as *Toshiyori Zuino* containing essays on poetry in 1113 CE.

Fujiwara no Mototoshi (1060 - 1142)

Mototoshi and Toshiyori were together the leading and characteristic poets of the Insei Period (1086 - 1185). He is included as one of the Six Late Classical Poetic Immortals and contributed a hundred and five poems to the *Kin'yoshu* and later imperial anthologies. A private collection of poetry of him also exists. He was the father of Bishop Kokaku for whom he composed the poem included here.

Fujiwara no Tadamichi (1097 - 1164)

Hosshoji Nyudo Saki no Kanpaku Daijodaijin Fujiwara no Tadamichi gained his high office from his father Tadazane becoming a Kanpaku in 1121. When Emperor Sutoku ascended the throne, he became a Regent in 1123 and then again in 1141 at the accession of Konoe. Tadamichi had an active role in the Hogen Rebellion of 1156 having supported Toba's son Masahito's (future Emperor GoShirakawa) claim to the throne against his brother Yorinaga who supported Sutoku's re-accession. Tadamichi was a greatly acclaimed poet and was the recipient of the previous poem. He was the father of the poet Jien (poem 95). He had a collection of poetry in Chinese named the *Hosshoji Kanpaku-shu* and one in Japanese called the *Tadamichi-shu*. All together, he contributed fifty-eight poems to the Imperial anthologies including the *Kin'yoshu*.

Retired Emperor Sutoku (1119 - 1164)

Emperor Sutoku reigned from 1123 to 1141 as the seventy-fifth emperor of Japan succeeding his father Emperor Toba at the age of five. He was however forced to abdicate in favour of his younger brother Konoe. After Konoe's death, Toba placed another of his sons, GoShirakawa on the throne instead of reinstating Sutoku and their conflict culminated in the Hogen Rebellion in 1156. Sutoku lost and was banished to the Sanuki province of Shikoku where he died in 1164. He was a lover of poetry and held several poetry competitions. He ordered Akisuke (poem 79) to compile the sixth imperial anthology--the *Shika-shu* and contributed seventy-eight poems to it and later imperial anthologies.

Minamoto no Kanemasa (?)

Kanemasa was a poet, scholar and *Kuge* (bureaucrat) at the late Heian court. His exact dates are unknown but he is found to be active till 1128. He participated in several poetry-competitions from 1110 to 1119 and was particularly close to Emperor Horikawa and Fujiwara no Tadamichi. He has several of his poems included in the *Kin'yoshu,* the *Shika Waka-shu,* the *Senzai Waka-shu,* the *Senzenzai Waka-shu* etc.

Fujiwara no Akisuke (1090 - 1155)

Akisuke, was a court poet, scholar and *kuge* at the Imperial Court and was particularly associated with Emperor Shirakawa He was the son of Akisue and the father of Fujiwara no Kiyosuke. He gained prominence sometime around 1100 CE and was promoted to the rank of *Jusanmi* in 1122 After Shirakawa's death, in 1129, he became *Sakyo-Daibu* and then the *shosanmi* in 1148. As a poet, Akisuke participated in several poetry competitions and was commissioned by the Emperor to compile the *Shika Waka-shu* in 1151. He has several of his poems included in the *Kin'yoshu* and a personal collection of poems called the *Daibu Akisuke Sakyo-dono-Shu* also exists.

Lady Horikawa (?)

Takienmon-In no Horikawa or Horikawa of the Takienmon-In was the daughter of Minamoto no Akinaka and served as Emperor Toba's consort and was the mother of Emperor Sutoku. She is a member of the Six Late Classical Poetic Immortals and has about sixty-six poems in the *Kin'yoshu* and later imperial anthologies. She also had a personal collection of poems which was, in a way, the fashion of her times.

Fujiwara no Sanesada (1139 - 1191)

Sanesada, also known as *GoTokudaijin Sadaijin Sanesada,* was the nephew of Shunzei and the first cousin of the compiler Fujiwara no Teika. He participated in several poetry-competitions and contributed seventy-eight poems to the *Senzai-shu* and later imperial anthologies. He also possessed a personal collection of poems called the *Rinka-shu.*

Doin (1090 - 1182)

Doin, before taking tonsure was known as Fujiwara no Atsuyori. He was the son of Kiyotaka and served at the Enryakuji Temple. He participated in several *utawase(s)* and rose to fame sometime between in the 1160s and 70s. He was a member of the Karin-in poetry circle.

Fujiwara no Shunzei (1114 - 1204)

Fujiwara no Shunzei, also known as Fujiwara no Toshinari or Shakua is one of the most important men in the Hyakunin Isshu being the father of the compiler--Teika. In his childhood he was given the name Akihiro but he later changed it to Shunzei in 1167. He was an innovative poet and liked to experiment with different forms. He was soon patronized by Emperor GoShirakawa and went on to compile the seventh imperial anthology, the *Senzai Waka-shu* in 1183. He worked as the "Chamberlain to the Empress Dowager"--a post that is said to be "pitiably low" but still managed to climb his way up to compile the anthology--an act of great esteem. Shunzei is said to have started composing poetry at a very young age which was probably the influence of his forefather's who were all esteemed poets. He usually preferred a fusion between old poetry styles, such as the ones seen in the Man'yoshu and the new styles imported from T'ang China. He was a lover of Murasaki's Tale of Genji and was also seen as a great critic of poetry. He usually preferred the orthodox style known as *"yugen"* which involved the "conveying of romantic emotions, with characteristic undertones of nostalgia and regret" and this trend is also to a certain degree, seen in Teika's style. His style is best described as a combination of charm, depth and mystery and a very appropriate configuration of words.

Fujiwara no Kiyosuke (1104 - 1177)

Kiyosuke was the second son of Akisuke (poem 79). He is said to have frequently disagreed with his father over poetry-styles. But eventually he became the leader of the Rokujo School of Poetry and received imperial patronage. Under Emperor Nijo's sanction he compiled the *Shoku Shika-shu*, but the emperor died before it was completed and thus the anthology failed to become as imperial one. Kiyosuke came to be revered for his works on poetry especially for the *Ogi Sho* and *Fukuro-Zoshi*. He has ninety-four poems in the *Senzai-shu* and later imperial anthologies, a personal collection of his poetry is also extant. He is also one of the Thirty-Six Late Classical Poetry Immortals.

Shun'e (1113 - ?)

Shun'e Hoshi was the son of Minamoto no Toshiyori (poem 74) and lived in a place called the 'The Garden in the Poetic Woods' called Karin-in. There he held several meeting and competitions on poetry. Among his students was the famous *Chomei* who recorded his words in the *Mumyo-Sho*. He contributed eighty-three poems to the various imperial anthologies and claimed his place among the Thirty-Six Late Classical Poetry Immortals. His personal collection of poetry is called the *Rin'yo Shu*.

Priest Saigyo (1118 - 1190)

Saigyo's original name was *Sato Norikiyo*. He was born in Kyoto and lived through the terrible periods of change. He took tonsure at the age of twenty-three and came to be known as En'i. Before that, we worked as a guard to the retired Emperor Toba. After taking tonsure, he lived at many places including Saga, Mt. Koga, Mt. Yoshino and Ise.

But he is most famous for his poetic journeys to the north of Honshu that later inspired Matsuo Basho. He was a good friend of Teika and contributed 266 poems to the various anthologies including his own, known as *Sank-shu*. Saigyo's poetry is filled with melancholy, sadness, loneliness and the imagery of desolation. He died in the Hirokawa Temple in Kawachi Province (modern Osaka Prefecture.)

Jakuren (1139 - 1202)

Jakuren was originally known as Sadanaga and was the adopted son of Fujiwara no Shunzei upon the death of Shunzei's younger brother. But after the birth of Teika and his brother, Sadanaga was forced to step aside from his claim to be the heir to Shunzei. After this he became a Buddhist monk and acquired the religious name 'Jakuren'. Following Saigyo's example, he went around on a journey as a wandering monk and composed poems. He was one of the six compilers of the eighth imperial anthology, the *Shin Kokin Waka-shu* and was particularly close to Teika. Thirty-five of his poems were included in the *Shin Kokin-shu* and one for the Hyakunin Isshu. Before he died, he adopted Fujiwara no Ietaka, one of the followers of Saigyo Hoshi.

Lady Betto

Lady Betto, mentioned as '*Kokamon-In no Betto*' was the service to Emperor Sutoku's empress Seishi who was later known as Kokamon. She was the daughter of Minamoto no Toshitaka. She has only nine poems in the imperial anthologies including the *Senzai-shu*.

Shokushi Naishinno (? - 1201)

Princess Shokushi was the third daughter of Emperor Go-Shirakawa living and working during the late Heian and early Kamakura periods. In 1159, she went entered service at the Kamo shrine as the high-priestess. After a few years, she left and took tonsure as a Buddhist nun. She contributed about forty-nine poems to the *Shin Kokin Waka-shu* and some others to the *Senzai Waka-shu*. Her name is also read as Shikishi, Shikiko as well as Noriko due to differential reading of the Kanji characters.

Inpumon In no Taifu (ca. 1131 - 1200)

Taifu was the daughter of Fujiwara no Nobunari and lived sometime between the dates mentioned above. She served Emperor Go-Shirakawa's daughter Princess Ryoshi who was also called by the name Inpumon-In. She was also a member of the Karin-en poetry circle and participated in many poetry competitions held there. She has thirty-six poems in the *Senzai Waka-shu* and later anthologies and also a personal collection of poems.

Fujiwara no Yoshitsune (1169 - 1206)

Fujiwara no Yoshitsune also known as, Kujo Yoshitsune was a court noble, i.e. *Kuge* in the late Heian and early Kamakura period. He was the son of Kujo Kanezane and held the position of *Sessho* or Regent at the imperial court.

Nijo-in no Taifu (1141 - 1217)

Nijo-in no Sanuki was the daughter of Minamoto no Yorimasa and was a maid-of-honor to Emperor Nijo. After Nijo's death in 1165, married Fujiwara no Shigeyuki. In 1190, she entered the service of Empress Ninshi, wife of Emperor Go-Toba but resigned to become a Buddhist nun six years later. she was one of the most respected female poets of her times and attended the poetry circles of Emperor Go-Toba and Emperor Juntoku. Many of her poems have been included in the imperial anthologies among which the most important is the *Senzai Waka-shu*. She is also one of the Thirty-Six Poetry Immortals.

Minamoto no Sanetomo (1192 - 1219)

Minamoto no Sanetomo is again one of the very important persons in Japanses history as well as the Ogura Hyakunin Isshu. He was the third *Shogun* of the Kamakura shogunate and the son of the founder, Minamoto no Yoritomo. Originally his name was *Senman* but he later changed it to Sanetomo. Sanetomo was also the last head of the Minamoto clan.

He lived a life of extreme chaos, since the death of Yoritomo in 1199. His maternal grandfather Hojo no Takamasa having usurped all political power, the *shogun* was reduced to the status of a non-functional head. Sanetomo's elder brother *Yoriie* was appointed *shogun* in 1202 but was soon stripped of his post and put under house arrest for plotting against the Hojo dominance and in 1204 he was assassinated. In 1203, Sanetomo was appointed as the *Shogun* as well as the leader of the Minamoto clan. But this appointment scarred Sanetomo's life forever. While his mother Hojo Masako used him merely as a pawn in her war against Tokimasa, Tokimasa tried to dethrone his grandson several times since 1205. This tug-of-war left Sanetomo in fear of losing his life.

Fearing a similar fate as his brother's, Sanetomo stopped interfering in political matters and diverted all his attention towards composing *waka*. He was a poetry student of Teika and composed some 700 poems between ages 17 and 22. His private collection of poetry was called *Kinkai Waka-shu*. He achieved the third highest position in the imperial court (that of the *udaijin*) but soon he collapsed into absolute inactivity being overcome by a fear of his own assassination. Finally, on the 13th of February, 1219 CE, Sanetomo was assassinated by his nephew Minamoto no Yoshinari while coming down the steps of the *Tsuragaoka Hachiman-gu* shrine after attending the celebrations for his nomination as the *udaijin*. However, after attending the celebrations for his nomination for the post of *udaijin*, while coming down the steps of the *Tsuragaoka Hachiman-gu* shrine in Kamakura, Sanetomo was ambushed and killed by his nephew Minamoto no Yoshinari on February 13th, 1219 CE. A few hours later Yoshinari was also beheaded for this deed thus bringing the Seiwa Genji line of the Minamoto clan and their rule over the *shogunate* to a sudden end.

Asukai no Masatsune (1170 - 1221)

Masatsune was the son of Nanbai Yoritsune and a member of the Asukai branch of the Fujiwara clan. He was renowned for his skills in both poetic compositions as well as playing *kemari* (a Japanese ball-game). He served under three Emperors, Emperor Go-Toba, Tsuchimikado and Emperor Juntoku. He studied poetry under Shunzei and had a personal collection of poems entitled *"Asukai-shu"* and has twenty-two poems included in the *Shin Kokin-Waka-shu* and also served as one of its compilers. A total of 134 of his poems have been included in the various anthologies. Probably by virtue of them, he succeeded in entering the service in the Poetry Bureau (*waka-dokoro*) working there 1201 onward.

Abbot Jien (1155 - 1225)

Jien belonged to the Fujiwara clan and was the son of Fujiwara no Tadamichi. He is known for being a Buddhist monk, historian and a *waka* poet of the late Heian and early Kamakura period. He joined the Tendai sect of Buddhism early in his life with the name *Dokaie* but later changed it to Jien. Ultimately he gained the rank of a *Daisojo* ('archbishop' and the head of the Tendai sect.) His masterpiece is a collection of essays on Japanese history entitled *"Gukansho"* (meaning "The Jottings of A Fool"). Jien however, as opposed to other historians and even the modern views on Japanese history considered the Feudal period as necessary for progress and all throughout his work supported the *Shogun's* claim to power. As a poet he is the second-most heavily represented poet in the *Shin Kokin Waka-shu* and also is one of the Thirty-Six New Poetry Immortals of Japan.

Saionji Kintsune (1171 - 1244)

Fujiwara no Kintsune, founder of the *Saionji* branch of the illustrious clan held the position of '*Nyudo Saki no Daijo Daijin*'. Through marital relations, he became the grandfather of the *shogun* Minamoto no Yoristune and received great political importance. Teika also enjoyed his patronage being married to his elder sister. He was an active poet in the court-poetry circles and is heavily represented in the *Shin Chokusen-shu* edited by Teika. He has 114 poems included in the *Shin Kokin Waka-shu* and other imperial anthologies.

Fujiwara no Teika (1162 - 1241)

Fujiwara no Sadaie, more popularly known as Fujiwara no Teika was the jewel of the late Heian period. He was a *waka* poet, critic, calligrapher, novelist, anthologist and scribe in the late Heian and early Kamakura period. He is counted as one of the greatest masters of the *waka* form of poetry and a truly genius anthologist. He was born to the illustrious Fujiwara no Shunzei who garnered his poetic abilities and allowed his genius to blossom; he further received a boost when he was patronized by Emperor Go-Toba and receiving sanctions to compile anthologies for him. His ideas and ideals on poetry continues to flourish and be studied even in the modern periods.

As a poet, Teika was extremely well-accomplished and his idea of "*Yoen*" or 'ethereal beauty' was highly praised during his lifetime. In poetry, Teika applied traditional language in an innovative way and this was greatly praised by Emperor Go-Toba who was himself a poetically inclined person and held frequent poetry competitions. Go-Toba employed him to compile the eighth imperial anthology, the *Shin Kokin Waka-shu* (1205) and in 1232, he was appointed the sole compiler of the *Shin Chokusen-shu*, the ninth imperial anthology. Scholars claim that the tremendous inner conflict that Teika went through in his 40s had caused a permanent change in his poetry style which was disliked by the Emperor. This caused his severe problems as he lost his position in court die to this conflict. They openly criticised each other through poetry and even denounced each other's beliefs. This led to Teika's unfortunate banishment but he soon found a supporter and patron in Go-Toba's son, the Emperor Juntoku, the poet with whom Teika concludes his Hyakunin Isshu. Other compilations and compositions of Teika include the "*Eiga taigai*" (1216), the '*Shuka no Daitai*', the '*Kindai Shuka*' and his diary, the '*Meigitusho*'.

Fujiwara no Ietaka (1158 - 1237)

Ietaka was a Japanese *waka* poet active in the Kamakura period. He is known to be a student of Fujiwara no Shunzei and was related to Jakuren by marriage ties. He is found to have participated in a great number of poetic-competitions and also had a personal collection of poems named the "*Gyokugin-shu*" i.e. "Collection of Jeweled Songs."

Emperor Go-Toba (1180 - 1239)

Emperor Go-Toba (named after Emperor Toba, Go-Toba literally means the later Emperor Toba), was the 82nd Emperor of Japan according to the Traditional Order of Succession reigning from 1183 to 1198. He was in close contact with Fujiwara no Teika and patronized him. Therefore, finding his poem in Teika's anthology is not at all surprising. His personal name (or imina) was *Takahira-shinno* and was the fourth son of Emperor Takakura and grandson to Emperor Go-Shirakawa.

Emperor Go-Toba had to take the throne at the tender age of three due to political insurgencies in the capital. In 1292, after Go-Shirakawa's death, the *shogunate* was established and the Emperor became a mere figurehead in the political scenario. Soon, in 1198, he was forced to abdicate by the *Shogun*. Though two of Go-Toba's sons assumed the throne, they were all soon forced to abdicate and the status of the Emperor fell drastically. In 1221, when the three year old grandson of Go-Toba was installed on the throne as Emperor Chukyo, the retired Go-Toba opposed it and prepared to stage a rebellion to overthrow the *Shogunate*. Though the samurais around Kyoto supported him, most of the warriors outside the Emperor's sphere of direct influence supported the *shogun* for personal gains and thus the rebellion known as the *Jokyu War* ended in Go-Toba's defeat and a nephew of Go-Toba's, being installed on the throne as Emperor Go-Horikawa replacing Emperor Chokyu. The emperor was banished to the distant isle of Oki and died there in 1239.

Though his political career was unfortunate, Emperor Go-Toba fostered his talent in multiple other niches. He was an ardent lover of swordsmanship, patronized swordsmen and himself became a master in the craft. He went on to become an acclaimed painter, musician, poet, critic and even an editor after he abdicated at the age of eighteen. As a poet, his greatest contribution is sanctioning the *Shin Kokin Waka-shu* and revival of the Poetry Bureau to power. It is said that the emperor himself took part in the compilation of the Shin Kokin-shu. He held several poetry competitions and composed numerous poems himself. Even after his exile, he continued to compose *waka* and even edited the Shin Kokin-shu to a great extent. His personal edition now called the *Oki-bon Shin Kokin-shu* (Oki edition) was completed and authorized in 1216. Among his other literary works is a criticism of aesthetics called the "Secret Teachings" or *Go-Toba no In Gokuden*. This particular text deals with great detail the complex relationship between the emperor and Fujiwara no Teika--the compiler of the Ogura Hyakunin Isshu.

Emperor Juntoku (1197 - 1242)

Juntoku was the 84th emperor of Japan, reigning from 1210 through 1221 according to the Traditional Order of Succession. Juntoku was the second son of Emperor Go-Toba and received the succession after his elder brother Emperor Tsuchimikado abdicated in 1210. However, due to his involvement in the Jokyu Rebellion of 1221, he was forced to abdicate that very year and was sent to the Isle of Sado in exile. He remained at Sado until his death in 1242 and was called *Sado-no-In* during his residence in Sado. Though Juntoku did not have a poetic legacy as vibrant as his father, he was tutored by Fujiwara no Teika whereby he selected one of Juntoku's poems for inclusion in the Ogura Hyakunin Isshu aptly ending it with a melancholic tone that characterized the air of the time.

Important Notes

[1] **Taika Reforms**: The Taika Reforms or the *"Taika no Kaishin"* meaning Great Reforms were a set of doctrines promulgated by Emperor Kotoku in 645 CE, these reforms were jointly drawn up by Prince Naka no Oe (Emperor Tenji), Emperor Kotoku and the Fujiwara progenitor Nakatomi no Kamatari at the after defeating the Soga clan and uniting Japan; and marked the end of the Asuka period. These reforms starting with simple land-reforms ultimately laid down the foundation of Japanese society encompassing all fields of arts, culture, language etc. Perhaps the most important feature of this edict that that it clearly stated that the Emperor was no more a clan-leader but a sovereign by the Mandate of Heaven, and also laying the foundation of Japanese bureaucracy following the Chinese model.

[2] **Mt. Kaguyama**: Kaguyama is a mountain often sung to in old poetry, situated in the south-east of the Nara basin. This mountain is often related with mysterious legends and is said that Jimmu Tenno, leaving his native land in Kyushu, and defeating his enemies had worshiped the Heavenly Deities, here at Mount Kaguyama before ascending the throne as the first Emperor of Japan at this very place. Thus making Kaguyama an extremely important place for Japanese imperial family and their claim to the throne.

[3] **Legend of Tanabata**: The legend of Tanabata relates the story of the Weaving Princess, *Orihime* and the Cow-herder Star *Hikoboshi*. Orihime was the daughter of the

King of the Skies and used to weave a fine silk (clouds) decorating the sky. Weary of her job, one day she decided to stroll around the place when she met Hikoboshi. Hikoboshi showed her around and amused her so much that she forgot to return home. Being worried the King of the Skies sent out a number of magpies to search for her but she shooed them away. Finally, the enraged king came and drove her back to her quarters destroying the only bridge that lay on the Heavenly River (the Milky Way) connecting Orihime and Hikoboshi's realms. Thus unable to meet the boy, Orihime was distraught. Pitying her, a band of sympathetic magpies built a bridge over the river by their flights and let Orihime pass to the other side of the river to meet Hikoboshi. This happens every year on the day of the Festival of Tanabata (7th July or August) which celebrates Orihime's reunion with Hikoboshi for one day. But the ending of the celebration also starts another year of waiting.

[4] **Gosechi Festival**: The Gosechi festival or *Gosechi no Mai* is actually a dance performance performed during the *Toyoakari no Sechie* festival. It began when the heavenly maidens brought down by the Sound of the *koto* of Emperor Temmu danced and waived to him five times during his legendary visit to Yoshino.

[5] **Mount Tsubaka**: Mount Tsubaka (877 m) is a double-peaked mountain located near Tsubaka, Ibaraki Prefecture, Japan. It is one of the most famous mountains in Japan particularly for its twin-peaks-- *Nyotai* and *Nantai*. Its summit presents a panoramic view of the entire Kanto plain. Legend has it that thousands of years ago, a deity descended from the

heavens and asked two mountains for a place to spend the night. Mt. Fuji refused, believing with pride and arrogance that it does not need the deity's blessings. Tsukuba, on the other hand, humbly welcomed the honored guest, even offering food and water. Today, Mt. Fuji is a cold, lonely, and barren mountain, while Mt. Tsukuba bursts with vegetation and is filled with colors as the seasons change.

[6] **Poetic Figures of Speech**: The poetic devices *Jokotoba*, *Kakekotoba* and Pillow words or *Makurakotoba* are most extensively used throughout the text in various ways. Jokotoba are preface-words used before certain nouns sometimes as hyperbole or even epithets. They are used for word-play employing metaphors and similes. *Makurakotoba* are slightly different as they have a strict syllable constrain. Jokotoba are more free and more creative in their senses as compared to Makurakotoba(s). *Kakekotoba*(s) on the other hand are pivot-words used to increase the poetic value of a poem. They are words like "matsu" which may both mean a pine tree as well as "to wait".

[7] **Lord Meng-Chang's Escape**: Lord Meng-Chang (d. ca. 280 BCE) a state official of the state of Qi during his travels in the State of Wei, he was captured and escaping the prison at night he reached *Hangu* barrier gate and found it close because it was still night-time. His enemy was approaching fast and in desperation he asked one of his vassals to imitate the crowing of a rooster. Upon hearing that cry, the guards of the gate thought that it was already dawning and opened the gate whereby Lord Meng-Chang escaped successfully.

[8] *Ausaka-no-Seki*: The gate of Osaka which actually refers to the Kanko barrier gate. It later became a symbol of the difficulty in meeting for secret lovers.

[9] **Hanami Festival**: Hanami festival is the traditional Japanese festival of flower viewing in which people enjoy the transient beauty of flowers particularly the *sakura* (cherry blossoms) and the *ume* (i.e. Plum blossoms). It is accompanied by singing and drinking of *sake* beneath the trees covered with flowers. Hanami is a centuries old festival and even finds mention in the *Tale of Genji*. Sakura was used the divine the year's harvest as well as to predict the coming of the season for rice-plantation thus making it extremely important. People also believed that there were *kami(s)* or divine spirits inside the trees and thus made offerings to it. Emperor Saga adopted this practice and started to celebrate Hanami in the Imperial Palace at Kyoto itself thereby elevating it to a different level. This ancient festival is still celebrated with equal enthusiasm although today the food and the sake has gradually become the main attraction instead of the flowers themselves.

[10] **The Hogen Rebellion**: The Hogen Rebellion is a short civil war fought between 28th July and 16th August, 1156 in order to resolve a dispute regarding succession within the Imperial family. It occurred when former Emperor Sutoku reclaimed the throne after his son's death against his brother Go-Shirakawa's claim. It was complicated because of the involvements of the Fujiwara(s) and the samurai clans. Fujiwara no Tadamichi sided with Go-Shirakawa against his brother Fujiwara no Yorinaga who supported Emperor

Sutoku. They in turn beckoned the Minamoto and Taira samurai clans for help who later gave shape to the rebellion and enthroned Emperor Go-Shirakawa banishing Sutoku to the Sanuki Province of Shikoku. As a result of this rebellion, a large part of Kyoto was damaged and disturbances became frequent. The former peace was destroyed and caused a drastic fall in the powers of the Emperor. The samurai(s) came to monopolize power and the Taira and the Minamoto became the all-powerful samurai leaders of Japan-- they will form the military governments of the future.

[11] **The Genpei War**: The Genpei war is yet another five year long civil war (1180 - 1185) fought between the Taira and the Minamoto clans leading to the downfall of the Taira and the establishment of the Minamoto Shogunate in Kamakura. The conflict between the two clans resurfaces when they were embroiled in yet another succession conflict. The Taira clan had already falled from power when Emperor Go-Shirakawa being strongly against the Taira launched a *coup d'etat* to remove prime minister Kiyomori from power. Iyomori was defeated and his capital was shifted to Fukuhara or Kobe. After Emperor Takakura's abdication, Daijo-daijin Taira no Kiyomori installed the 3 year old grandson Antoku on the throne, hoping to regain the lost power. This enraged Go-Shirakawa's son Prince Michihito. When the latter asked for Minamoto support and contested the nomination, the seeds of the conflict were sown.

[12] **Bo-Juyi**: Bo Juyi or Bai Juyi (772 - 846) was a Chinese poet and official of the middle T'ang dynasty. He

passed the Civil Service examinations in 800 and was made a member of the Hanlin Academy and he also served as the Assistant Secretary to the Prince's Tutor since 814. Getting himself embroiled in some conflicts at court he was exiled only to return to the capital in 819 as the new Second class Assistant Secretary. He received several posts such as Governor of the Provinces of Hangzhou, Suzhou etc. Retiring in 839 after suffering from a paralytic attack. One of the most prolific of the Tang poets, Bo Juyi wrote over 2,800 poems, which he had copied and distributed to ensure their survival. They are notable for their relative accessibility. It is said that he would rewrite any part of a poem if one of his servants was unable to understand it. The accessibility of Bo Juyi's poems made them extremely popular in his lifetime, in both China and Japan, and they continue to be read in these countries today. Bo Juyi was known for his interest in the old *yuefu* form of poetry, which was a typical form of Han poetry, namely folk ballad verses, collected or written by the Music Bureau. These were often a form of social protest. And, in fact, writing poetry to promote social progress was explicitly one of his objectives. He is also known for his well-written poems in the regulated verse style. He is particularly known for the composition of the long poem *changhen-ge* or The Song of Everlasting Regret.

[13] **The House of Mikohidari**: A minor branch of the Fujiwara clan descending from Fujiwara no Michinaga through his sixth son Nagaie (1005 - 1064). Teika was a member of this branch of the clan.

[14] **The Garden in the Poetic Forests**: Known as the Karin'en poetry circle this was a large society of poets active during the two decades after 1150 organized by monk Shun'e. They met monthly and discussed poetry and even held competitions. Some forty poets were its members. Besides their activities in Shun-e's house, they also organized poetic pilgrimages to the tombs of Narihira or Hitomaro--a poet revered by the members of this society. It acted as a free zone for poets who were members of other schools of poetry that competed against each other for supremacy.

[15] **List of the Imperial Anthologies**:

Nara Period	:	*Man'yoshu* (AD 785)
Heian Period	:	*Kokin Waka-shu* ordered by Emperor Daigo. 905 CE
		Gosen Waka-shu ordered by Emperor Murakami.951 CE.
		Shui Waka-shu ordered by Emperor Kazan.
		GoShui Waka-shu ordered by Emperor Shirakawa. 1086.
		Kin'yo Waka-shu ordered by Retired Emperor Shirakawa. 1124-27.
		Shika Waka-shu ordered by Emperor Sutoku. 1154.
		Senzai Waka-shu ordered by Emperor Go-Shirakawa. 1188.
		Shin Kokin Waka-shu ordered by Emperor Go-Toba. 1201.

Bibliography

[1] Mostow, Joshua S., *Picture of the Heart: The Hyakunin Isshu in Word and Image,* Hawaii University Press, 1994. Print.

[2] Porter, William N., *A Hundred Verses from Old Japan,* Oxford, Clarendon Press, 1909. Print.

[3] McMillan, Peter, *One Hundred Poets, One Poem Each: A Translation of the Ogura Hyakunin Isshu,* Columbia University Press, 2008. Print.

[4] McCauley, Clay, *Hyakunin Isshu (Single Songs of a Hundred Poets),* Kelly and Walsh, 1917. Print.

[5] Shonagon, Sei, *The Pillow Book,* Translated by Meredith McKinney, Penguin Classics, Penguin Publishers, 2006. Print.

[6] Seindensticker, Edward (Tr.), *The Gossamer Years: The Diary of a Noblewoman of Heian Japan,* Turtle Publishing, 1964. Print.

[7] "https://en.wikipedia.org/wiki/Ogura_Hyakunin_Isshu". Web.

[8] "http://onethousandsummers.blogspot.in/p/chouyaku-hyakuninisshu.html". Web.

[9] "https://100poets.wordpress.com", Web.

[10] Nobutaka Inoue, Endo Jun, Mori Mizue, Ito Satori (ed.), *KAGU: Shinto: A Short History*, London: 2003, RoutledgeCurzon. Print.

[11] Suzuki, Daisetz T., *Zen and Japanese Culture*, Princeton University Press, 1938.

[12] Rodd, Laurel Rasplica (Tr.), *Kokinshu: A Collection of Poems Ancient and Modern"*, Princeton University Press, 1984. Print.

[13] Waley, Arthur, *"Japanese Poetry: The Uta"*, London: 1946, Lund, Humphries & Co. Print.

Printed in the United States
By Bookmasters